Suffolk
WATERSIDE WALKS

Geoff Pratt

COUNTRYSIDE BOOKS

NEWBURY, BERKSHIRE

First published 1999
© Geoff Pratt 1999

COUNTRYSIDE BOOKS
3 Catherine Road
Newbury, Berkshire

ISBN 1 85306 568 4

*For Jean Elizabeth Pratt, with whom the book
was planned and developed, and who died
on 14 February 1998. For almost 45 years
she was my close companion, active partner
and loving wife.*

Designed by Graham Whiteman
Cover illustration by Colin Doggett
Maps and photographs by the author

Produced through MRM Associates Ltd., Reading
Typeset by Techniset Typesetters, Newton-le-Willows
Printed by J. W. Arrowsmith Ltd., Bristol

Contents

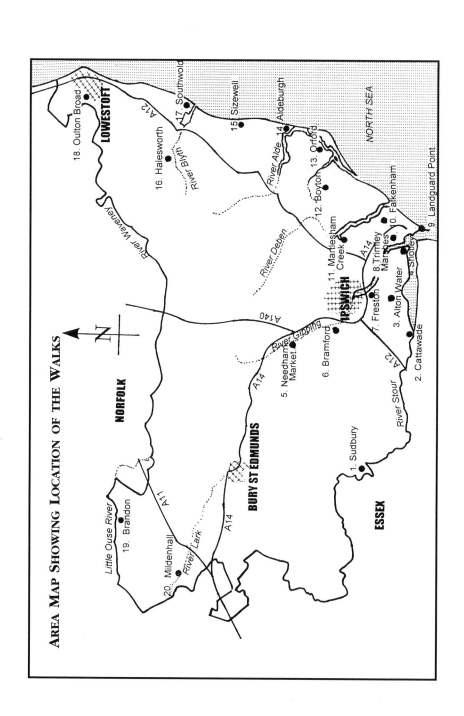

AREA MAP SHOWING LOCATION OF THE WALKS

N

NORFOLK

BURY ST EDMUNDS

ESSEX

LOWESTOFT

IPSWICH

NORTH SEA

River Waveney

Little Ouse River

River Lark

A11

A14

A14

A140

A12

A14

River Stour

River Gipping

River Deben

River Blyth

River Alde

A12

1. Sudbury
2. Cattawade
3. Alton Water
4. Shotley
5. Needham Market
6. Bramford
7. Freston
8. Trimley Marshes
9. Landguard Point
10. Falkenham
11. Martlesham Creek
12. Boyton
13. Orford
14. Aldeburgh
15. Sizewell
16. Halesworth
17. Southwold
18. Oulton Broad
19. Brandon
20. Mildenhall

Walk

PUBLISHER'S NOTE

We hope that you obtain considerable enjoyment from this book; great care has been taken in its preparation. Although at the time of publication all routes followed public rights of way or permitted paths, diversion orders can be made and permissions withdrawn.

We cannot of course be held responsible for such diversion orders and any inaccuracies in the text which result from these or any other changes to the routes nor any damage which might result from walkers trespassing on private property. We are anxious though that all details covering the walks are kept up to date and would therefore welcome information from readers which would be relevant to future editions.

INTRODUCTION

Most people enjoy the waterside. I remember, as a child, the excitement of a seaside visit and the fun of splashing in the water. Adults too are attracted to the sea in all its moods; but not just the sea – tranquil lakes and gently flowing rivers are also a source of fascination and pleasure. In Suffolk we are fortunate that there are eight major rivers. Six of them flow eastward to the North Sea and the other two flow west, being tributaries of the Great Ouse River which discharges into The Wash. Where the eastbound rivers cross the wide flat coastal plain, they widen out to form extensive tidal estuaries. The North Sea coastline together with these tidal inlets is backed with a wide strip of light sandy heathland, much of which is given over to forestry.

Most of the walks in this book are through this area of shore, coastal marshes and sandy heath. In the summer months the river estuaries are an important recreational area for boating. Here sailing boats and motor cruisers travel up and down the waterways, stopping at the idyllic riverside villages and marinas. Large ocean going ships will be seen at the ports of Felixstowe and Harwich.

At all times, and particularly in winter when the small boats are absent, many species of duck, geese and wading birds will be seen and heard. Some flocks are resident, some migrants and others just passing through the area.

The other walks are along the banks of the upper reaches of the rivers where they flow through shallow valleys fringed by lush water meadows.

The walks described are along public rights of way or permissive paths. They are all circular and within the capacity of the average person, including those of mature years and families with young children. Apart from one, the routes are all between 2 miles and 7 miles and for the longer circuits I have suggested a shorter alternative if at all possible. The exception is a very special all-day walk of 10 miles along the River Alde from Orford. Wherever you are, please keep dogs under close control and comply with the Country Code.

The sketch maps which accompany each walk are intended to be a simple guide showing the starting point and the general direction. They are not to scale and do not necessarily give every detail of the route. It is always a good idea to take an Ordnance Survey map with you as well – these are particularly useful for identifying the main features of views – and I have included details of the relevant Landranger (1:50,000) or Pathfinder (1:25,000) sheets.

Likely places where cars can be safely parked are mentioned for each walk. Nevertheless readers are asked to park with care and never to obstruct a road or access way. Modern farm equipment is often of enormous size.

For refreshment, a nearby café or pub, which has been used by the author, is mentioned for each route. In most cases there are several establishments conveniently within range, and it should not be assumed that the unnamed premises are in any way unsuitable or inferior. Places of interest within easy driving distance of the walk area are also given, to help you plan a longer outing should you wish to do so.

The help received from many people is gratefully acknowledged, in particular Dick Leech and Doug Hart of the Ramblers' Association. Also Mr and Mrs Adams for permission to recommend their car park at Falkenham, and Mrs Ford of the River Stour Trust for helpful information.

Finally, thanks to Miss M. E. Bird and all the members of my family for encouragement and help.

Geoff Pratt

WALK 1
THE RIVER STOUR AT SUDBURY

*From the ancient market town of Sudbury this pleasant walk follows
the meandering River Stour upstream through lush water meadows.
You will pass three former watermills before returning along part of
the Valley Walk, a permissive path along the former railway line to
Lavenham and Bury St Edmunds.*

The Quay Theatre

Sudbury lies on the River Stour at the southern edge of Suffolk.
Many of the riverside meadows at the edge of the town are
commons with ancient and attractive names such as Freemen's Great
Common. These commons are criss-crossed with footpaths. The river
provided water-power and there were three watermills in a 2 mile
stretch of the river here.

From the early 18th century the River Stour was a navigable
waterway, and barges would carry local freight along the river as far
as Sudbury, until 1914 when the last barge trip was made.

There are several pubs, cafés and restaurants in the centre of

8

Sudbury. Prominent on the north side of Market Hill is the Black Boy. An interesting and changing menu includes pork steak in port and Stilton, spicy beef curry and mushroom stroganoff. Telephone: 01787 379046. The Quay Theatre, which is passed on the walk, has a pleasant coffee shop and café where meals are served.

- **HOW TO GET THERE:** Sudbury lies on the A134 Colchester to Bury St Edmunds road. From Ipswich and the east, use the A1071 through Hadleigh.
- **PARKING:** The start of the walk is at the Kingfisher Leisure Centre. From a roundabout at the eastern side of the town centre, take the minor road, Great Eastern Road, which leads to Station Road. At the end there is a large car park on the left.
- **LENGTH OF THE WALK:** 5 miles. Maps: OS Landranger sheet 155 Bury St Edmunds and Sudbury area; Pathfinder 1029 Sudbury and Lavenham (GR 876410).

THE WALK

1. From the Kingfisher Centre, go a few yards and leave the car park at its eastern side, through a pedestrian gate at the start of the Valley Walk. Bear right along the path for about 20 yards and then turn left over a steel bridge onto Friars Meadow. Keep straight on across the meadow and at the far side, reach the bank of the River Stour. Make almost a U-turn and walk beside the river on your left.

2. At the corner of the meadow, turn right beside a small tributary and make your way to a path under a former railway bridge. After 200 yards turn left through a kissing gate along a path which leads to the Sudbury Quay Theatre. Before the theatre, pass on the left The Granary, a fine old building, now the HQ of the River Stour Trust.

Go out past the theatre and turn right along Quay Lane. In 200 yards turn left at a road junction. Before long pass on the left the gatehouse of a 13th-century Dominican friary. Follow the main road as it bends left, then pass the Baptist church and bear right on a footpath through All Saints' churchyard and at the far side turn right along a road.

Reach a T-junction. Turn right, pass the Bull Hotel and in a few yards turn left down Noah's Ark Lane which soon narrows to a footpath and leads over a bridge, out to the meadows.

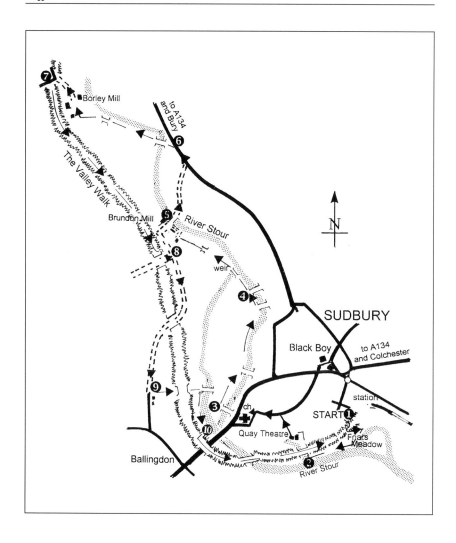

3. Turn right and walk beside the river on the right. Note, on the opposite bank, the gazebos on the wall looking out over the river and the water meadows. The river makes a right turn and here swing right towards the white painted mill, now the Mill Hotel. The mill stream flows out from under the building.

Leave the Freemans Great Common by a kissing gate at the corner of the Mill Hotel and turn left along the side of the building. Just beyond the hotel, the path is again following the bank of the river. After passing sluice gates, continue straight on with a children's play area on the left, and pass a wooden footbridge leading to a large green on the opposite bank.

4. In a further 200 yards keep on past a concrete bridge and, immediately beyond it, steps down into the river are the remains of a former bathing place. Bear slightly left on a grass path across the meadow and at the far side cross a bridge over an arm of the river. On the right is a weir and beside it a fish pass, a sort of ladder of small pools, which is a relic of the time when salmon were in the river.

Follow the track across another meadow to a bridge over a usually dried up watercourse, and continue towards a flint-faced cottage, and you will soon be walking beside a high brick garden wall on the right. Cross a stile and join a gravel drive. In a few yards, after a bend to the left, pass a row of pink painted weatherboarded cottages.

5. At a junction of tracks turn right beside Brundon Mill and immediately cross a bridge over the River Stour. Continue along a lane beside a wood on the left, and in 300 yards turn left along the Sudbury to Long Melford road.

6. Walk on the footway and in just over 200 yards turn left down a narrow lane between hedges. In 100 yards cross a timber cart-bridge, go through a kissing gate and walk straight across a meadow. At the far side negotiate another kissing gate and cross a bridge. Swing round to the right and follow a hedge on the right round the field.

The right of way is straight across the field as is indicated by the waymark on the bridge handrail. However, path users seem to keep beside the hedge on the right.

Some 25 yards before reaching a brick building on the right, turn right through a narrow gate beside a farm gate to enter a meadow planted with several trees. Bear slightly left, keeping well to the left of the white painted Borley Mill. Go through a narrow gate at the corner of the meadow and then follow a narrow path beside the high garden wall of Borley Hall, which leads to the entrance drive of Borley Mill.

Walk down the drive for 100 yards to a road junction. Make a U-turn to the left to join the Valley Walk along the former railway line.

7. Follow the good wide footpath of the Valley Walk. Cross a watercourse by a steel girder bridge and continue along the path. About 20 yards before a brick arch bridge over the track, climb steps up the embankment on the left and swing right at the top, to cross a stile out to a gravel farm track and turn left.

8. Just by some farm buildings turn right to go along a track between hedges. This is Brundon Lane. Soon you will have a good view across the meadows to Sudbury. Cross high over the Valley Walk on a brick bridge and continue along Brundon Lane.

9. After passing, on the right, the Anglian Water building, the road is surfaced. At the point where a kerbed footway starts on the left, turn left at a sign. Cross a steel bridge and then go half left towards a brick arch on the far side of the field.

Go through the arch and continue straight on to a steel bridge over the River Stour but do not cross it. Turn right at the riverside but go straight across the meadow to a steel gate, and enter a short lane, passing an old industrial building on the left.

10. Just before the road, and opposite a car park, turn right up an embankment to meet the Valley Walk again. Go left, first crossing the road and later crossing the river. Note, as you pass, a view of the Quay Theatre and return along the old railway line back to the start.

PLACES OF INTEREST NEARBY
Gainsborough's House is in Gainsborough Street, Sudbury. This is the birthplace of Thomas Gainsborough and, as well as being a museum housing furniture and other items of the period, it is an art gallery exhibiting a collection of his works. Exhibitions of contemporary art are also held here. Open Tuesdays to Saturdays 10 am to 5 pm; Sundays 2 pm to 5 pm (it closes at 4 pm from November to March). Telephone: 01787 372958.

WALK 2

THE RIVER STOUR BETWEEN CATTAWADE AND FLATFORD

This beautiful route through Constable country starts at Cattawade and follows the northern arm of the river. It passes the delightfully situated Willy Lott's cottage as well as picturesque Flatford Mill, and continues, if you wish to do the full route, to Fen Bridge. The return is beside the main arm of the Stour to finish overlooking the tidal estuary towards Manningtree and the quay at Mistley.

Flatford Mill

The River Stour forms the boundary between Suffolk and Essex for most of its length. This walk explores the lower reaches of the river to where it discharges, at Cattawade, into its long tidal estuary.

The river, flanked with lush water meadows, flows through a wide, shallow valley. John Constable, the famous landscape painter, lived and painted here. The National Trust at its complex of buildings at Flatford has an exhibition about Constable which includes photographs and maps identifying where he painted several of his well-known pictures.

The Stour was developed as a waterway in the early 18th century, and barges carried freight as far as Sudbury until 1914. The River Stour Trust was formed in 1968 to protect and enhance navigation along the river and the Trust's volunteers have restored Flatford Lock and other installations along the river.

At Flatford, the National Trust's Bridge Cottage Restaurant serves lunches and teas. There is a decidedly 18th-century ambience with the menu offering, for example, home made pottage, salamangundy (salad and pickles), painter's palette, with syllabub, as a sweet. The restaurant is open every day from May to September (10 am to 5.30 pm). At most other times it is open on Wednesdays to Sundays (11 am to 5.30 pm). Telephone: 01206 298260.

There are several pubs in East Bergholt.

- **HOW TO GET THERE:** Leave the A12 at the B1070 interchange and go towards East Bergholt. Continue through East Bergholt to Cattawade. Turn right at a brown 'Picnic Site' sign, 150 yards before the A137 junction.
- **PARKING:** There is a car park at the Cattawade picnic site.
- **LENGTH OF THE WALK:** 5 miles or 6½ miles. Maps: OS Landranger sheet 169 Ipswich and The Naze area, also a tiny part on 155 Bury St Edmunds and Sudbury area; Pathfinder 1053 Manningtree and Dedham (GR 100331).

THE WALK

1. From the Cattawade picnic site go out to the B1070 (East Bergholt) road and turn left along the footway. Pass a row of houses on the right and continue along the road passing Malting Cottage and Brantham Mill industrial estate.

2. After West Green Cottages, turn left along an access driveway. In less than 50 yards go right through a narrow gap in a hedge, beside a brick gate pier. Turn left and continue on a grassy headland with the hedge on the left. Before long, go through the hedge to walk a narrow path beside a wooden fence on the left. Eventually the path leads over a stile to the corner of a meadow, where, on the left, you will see an arm of the River Stour. Go straight on beside the hedge on the right. At the end of the meadow cross two stiles in close

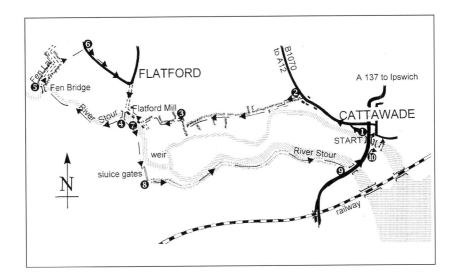

proximity and still go straight on, keeping beside the hedge on the right.

After crossing several similar fields come to a field corner. Turn right in accordance with a Stour Valley Path waymark, and walk towards an electricity pylon.

3. Swing left almost underneath the pylon, keeping beside the hedge on the left, and at the field corner cross a stile and bend left through thick vegetation. In a few yards turn right on a grass path between an old hedge on the right and a newly planted hedge on the left. In 200 yards the grass path bends right. Before long, at a corner, bend left, ignoring a kissing gate on the right.

The wide grass path ends at a junction of ways. Turn right along a gravel path which immediately passes the white painted Willy Lott's House. Continue along the well-used path beside Flatford Mill.

After passing, on the left, the old dry dock and the National Trust tea room and shop, go left beside thatched Bridge Cottage and cross the River Stour.

4. This is Flatford Bridge and at this point there is a choice. Those walking the 5 mile route should turn left beside the river and continue from point 7. Those wishing to follow the longer 6½ mile walk should go through the special wheelchair gate at the end of the bridge and walk through the meadows beside the river on the right. Keep beside the river and in a little over ¹/₂ mile, come to Fen Bridge, a timber bridge lifted into position by helicopter in 1985.

5. Having crossed the River Stour, walk up the leafy green lane. Cross a substantial cart bridge over a backwater of the river and in a further 50 yards where the lane bends to the left, go straight ahead over a steel stile, into a pasture. Bending a little to the right, climb the hill; the path is visible in the grass. At the top cross another steel stile, go over the narrow road and climb a bank opposite.

6. Immediately turn right between a fence and the roadside hedge. In a short time, cross a farm track and then continue as before on a footpath behind the hedge. Later walk along the narrow one-way road, and where it bends left, turn right into the car park and walk beside a hedge on the left. At the bottom of the car park, continue down a footpath to Bridge Cottage.

Turn right in front of Bridge Cottage and cross, for a second time, Flatford Bridge and turn left.

7. Having turned left, pass alongside Flatford Lock, which was restored by the River Stour Trust in 1991. Just beyond the lock, on the opposite bank, is Flatford Mill.

Keep along the well-used gravel path. The Stour is still on the left but meandering further away. Before long you reach a concrete structure comprising 36 sluice gates which in times of flood protect the meadows from flooding from the river whilst enabling surplus floodwater to drain back to the river. Go over steel steps attached to a farm gate and continue beside the sluices. Some people walk along the concrete walkway.

8. At the far end of the concrete sluice gates turn left along a footpath on top of a raised bank, still with the river on the left. Continue along the bank for just over a mile, crossing several stiles en route, and reach the busy A137 road.

9. Cross the road and turn left along the footway. In 100 yards cross the main arm of the Stour while passing, on the right, a range of seven large sluice gates which protect the river from abnormal high tides.

10. Keep beside the road and about 100 yards before reaching the 30 mph speed limit sign, go half right down a ramp to the old road. Immediately before old Cattawade Bridge, turn right and in 100 yards turn left over the river, passing more sluice gates. Just beyond the sluices cross a slipway with rollers whereby boats can transfer between the river and the sea, and follow the path out to a road at Cattawade village. Go left, pass the bridge again, on the left, and the Crown public house on the right. Immediately after the road swings right, turn left along a cul-de-sac, passing the Fontana (Chinese) Restaurant. At the end of the road keep on the footpath, cross the A137 and swing left, back to the Cattawade picnic site.

PLACES OF INTEREST NEARBY

There are interesting displays at the National Trust's *Bridge Cottage, Flatford* (telephone: 01206 298260). Nearby is the *Granary*, a privately owned museum of rural bygones. Boats for hire are available at Flatford and Dedham.

WALK 3
ALTON WATER AND THE STOUR ESTUARY

This is a delightful ramble along well-used tracks and footpaths, starting from lovely Alton Water, a haven for wildfowl. The walk continues to the River Stour at the head of Holbrook Creek. From this point there is an optional loop, following the river wall eastward to the edge of Harkstead. The final leg is westward along the Stour, to Stutton church and through the edge of Stutton village.

Holbrook Creek

Alton Water is a large reservoir constructed in the 1970s to serve Ipswich and the surrounding area. The lake, 3 miles long and up to ¼ mile wide, is now a major recreational site, with facilities for fishing, walking, cycling, sailing canoeing and many other activities. A mile to the south is the picturesque estuary of the River Stour. Here there are opportunities for bird watching and boating.

18

The tower of the Royal Hospital School stands out prominently in this area, and the clock chiming the quarter hours can be heard from far around. Originally founded at Greenwich, the school is now a co-educational boarding school providing education for the children of mariners.

The Compasses in Holbrook, just east of Alton Water, is a bright and attractive pub, serving a full range of meals. The blackboard shows what roast joint, what kind of puff pastry pie and what curry dish are on offer on the day. Two unusual decorative features are the pink ceiling and a collection of different key rings fixed to the picture rail. Telephone: 01473 328332.

A café overlooking Alton Water, at the Visitors' Centre by the car park, serves drink and light refreshments, such as Cornish pasties, sausage rolls, scones and cakes.

- **HOW TO GET THERE:** Leave the A14, the Ipswich Bypass, at the Wherstead Interchange and follow the A137 towards Manningtree. In 5 miles turn sharp left along the B1080 towards Holbrook. Just beyond the village of Stutton turn left at the entrance to the Alton Water site and reach the main car park in $1/4$ mile.
- **PARKING:** Use the Pay and Display car park at the Alton Water Visitors' Centre.
- **LENGTH OF THE WALK:** $4^1/2$ miles or 6 miles. Maps: Landranger sheet 169 Ipswich and The Naze area; Pathfinder 1053 Manningtree and Dedham (GR 155354).

THE WALK

1. From the car park continue along the access road, beside the lake on the left. Wander along the grassy margin of the lake.

On reaching the dam, go left through the commemorative gateway and cross the dam. Below it is the Water Treatment Plant whilst 100 yards away in the lake is the water draw-off tower.

2. At the far end of the dam, cross a bridge over the spillway and go straight on for about 50 yards. Turn right to take a 2 yard wide grass path beside the Treatment Plant fence, running downhill beside a plantation of larch trees on the right. Cross a stream in the valley bottom and continue through a small wood.

At a junction of paths leave the more heavily used path and keep straight on beside a stream with a chainlink fence on the right.

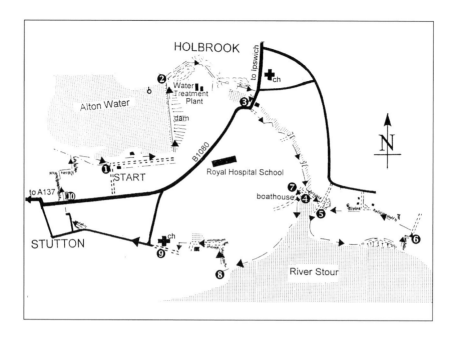

Before long, cross a stile into a willow plantation and follow the path which leads out through a gap beside a gate to a road. Turn right along the footway which soon becomes a wooden walkway beside a mill pond on the right, whilst on the left is the weatherboarded Holbrook Mill.

3. Where the causeway ends, turn left for a few yards, and go straight on along the footpath signed to River Stour, Lower Holbrook and Stutton church.

In a few yards leave the drive, which serves a bungalow, and take the narrow grass path between a hedge and a fence The path bends left and then right, to follow a stream, on the left. Continue along the footpath beside the watercourse for about 1/2 a mile.

4. On reaching a gravel track, those wishing to take the shorter walk (4½ miles), should turn right (and read on from point 7).

For the full walk, go left for 100 yards and turn right at a T-junction to follow the shore. Before long take the opportunity to bear right down a short ramp to see Holbrook Creek where a number of boats are moored.

5. Return to the path and continue beside the river wall, swinging gradually round to the left. There are fine views here to Manningtree and down towards Parkeston Quay and Harwich.

As you round the bend, the river wall merges into a low, soft cliff. The path follows the edge of the cliff which becomes higher and eventually you are walking with a wooded slope on the seaward side. Keep beside the wood round several bends but before long, at a corner, turn left away from the river, and climb a hill beside a wood on the right.

6. The path ends just by the gate to Gallister Cottage. Go left along the track for about 50 yards and then turn left along a cross-field path towards Holbrook Creek. Before long the path is following a hedge on the right and then, at a hedge corner, swing half left across the field to another hedge corner right beside a twin electricity pole. Go through a gap in a fence and cross straight over a gravel drive, as waymarked, and take a narrow path through a wooded area. In 50 yards, on leaving the trees, swing left to a three-way footpath sign and turn left onto a gravel track.

Where the track turns left, go straight on through a gap beside a red steel gate and immediately turn right following a hedge on the right. Keep on across the field, dropping down towards Holbrook Creek. On reaching the gravel track where you were earlier, turn right and in about 50 yards turn left, retracing your steps beside the creek. Pass the footpath on the right which you used earlier, and keep to the cinder track.

7. Swing left along the track at the head of the creek and after passing the school boathouse turn left onto the top of the river wall with the Royal Hospital School behind its extensive playing fields on the right.

8. After following the river wall for 1/2 mile descend steps leading down to the right and cross a wooden bridge. Continue beside a row of trees on the right to reach a green lane. Turn left.

Soon the lane becomes a gravel drive which, after passing a small duck pond on the right, swings left to a large house. Leave the track and go straight on across a well-tended grass field. At the far side turn left beside the edge of the churchyard of Stutton church and in a few yards swing rightish up to a road at the church entrance.

9. Pass the church on the right and then a large white farmhouse. Keep straight on at the road junction and in $\frac{1}{2}$ mile, immediately after passing a house called The Grove, turn right along a narrow, hedge lined footpath.

The path leads to a green in front of houses. Go left to the road and then right along the road to the far end of the cul-de-sac, where you will find a tarmac path which leads out to the road, the B1080.

10. Cross the road to a broad lane leading to a field. Keep straight on beside a hedge on the left. Go through a gap into the next field and follow the path to the right which leads over a stile into the Alton Water site. Turn right and follow the path back to the car park and the start.

PLACES OF INTEREST NEARBY

Cycles are available for hire at the *Alton Water Visitors' Centre* and there is a recognised cycle route around the lake. Telephone: 01473 328873. At *Alton Water Sports Centre* you can arrange hire of windsurfers and dinghies. Telephone: 01473 328408.

WALK 4
THE SHOTLEY PENINSULA

A variety of landscapes await you on this walk along the shoreline of the River Orwell – rolling farmland, wide salt marshes, and splendid views of the delightful River Stour. You can also visit Shotley church and half-timbered Shotley Hall before returning (choice of two routes) to the riverside.

The lock at Shotley Marina

The Shotley peninsula is an undulating area of farmland and woods, sandwiched between the River Stour and the River Orwell. Across the Stour, to the south, lies Harwich with its mainly passenger port of Parkeston Quay. To the east, are the container berths of Felixstowe.

At the start of the walk, at Shotley Gate, the Bristol Arms public house stands facing the Stour Estuary. Whilst offering a variety of other fare, it concentrates on fish dishes, for example prawn and mushroom pancake and ocean pie. Telephone: 01473 787200.

- **HOW TO GET THERE:** Leave the A14, the Ipswich Bypass, at the A137 (Wherstead) interchange. Follow the A137 towards Ipswich and at the first roundabout, turn right on the B1456 and continue for about 7 miles to the end of the road.
- **PARKING:** Park alongside the sea wall opposite the Bristol Arms. There is also a large car park at the Shotley Marina.
- **LENGTH OF THE WALK:** 5 miles or 6½ miles. Maps: OS Landranger sheet 169 Ipswich and The Naze area; Pathfinder 1054 Felixstowe and Harwich (GR 246336).

THE WALK

1. Starting at the end of the road, opposite the Bristol Arms, go east towards the Shotley Marina. On the right, across the water, is the town of Harwich. Walk along the sea wall and later continue beside the marina car park, to the lock gate.

Cross the lock gate and continue on a gravel path between the marina basin and the estuary. At the time of writing, there is a suggestion that the right of way may be diverted away from the lock gate. If this happens an alternative route will be well signed.

2. On reaching the end of the marina basin, continue northward along a narrow footpath on the top of the river wall. Shortly after the end of a fenced area, there is a white boundary stone beside the path. Keep along the river wall. Before long pass a grid of wooden stakes driven into the mud about ten years ago to counter erosion. Soon the river wall bears away from the water's edge and you come to an area of salt marsh on the right.

3. On reaching a point where the river wall merges into a small rounded hill, leave the River Orwell, descending the bank, and then keep beside a thick hedge on the right, through two pastures. A stile leads into a narrow lane. In 200 yards turn left along a stony lane and climb a little hill. At the top, just before the church, go right, up a concrete path, to look into the old cemetery where sailors, many being boys from the former training establishment HMS *Ganges*, are buried.

4. After passing the church, keep straight on at a crossroads. In ¼ mile come to timber-framed Shotley Hall, on the right.

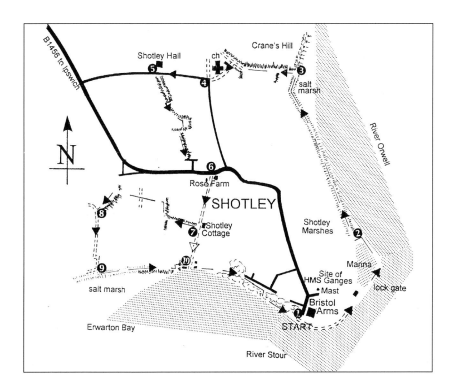

5. Opposite Shotley Hall turn left along a grass lane which in about 200 yards turns right, down a ramp, to a field. Swing left along the headland with a hedge on the left and about 50 yards before the corner of the field, turn right along a cross-field path towards a double electricity pole.

Cross a timber bridge and go 10 yards to the right and then left on a headland path with a hedge on the left. This leads up to a street, Garden Close. Turn left and immediately right along a road which soon meets the B1456 road where you turn left.

6. In 100 yards turn right at Rose Farm and follow a hard farm road for a little over ¼ mile to Shotley Cottage, an isolated large house. At this high point there is a magnificent view of the River Stour with the cranes of Parkeston Quay on the opposite shore.

For a short cut, go straight ahead along the farm road, to the river's edge, then turn left along the signed footpath and continue from point 10.

7. For the main walk, turn right at Shotley Cottage and follow a grass footpath. Soon you will be walking beside a trim hedge on the right. At the corner of the field go through a gap and turn right alongside the hedge for less than 200 yards. Turn left at a sign and take a well-used path across the field.

After crossing a cart track, continue, almost in the same direction, and at the far side, cross a stile and bear left beside a hedge on the left, passing several old sweet chestnut trees.

8. The path ends at a cart track. Bear left on the track which at first follows the edge of the field, but soon is a cross-field track towards the river. After a few bends the track comes to the river wall.

9. Climb the bank and turn left along it. In the distance, Shotley Pier and the Bristol Arms can be seen. Before long you are walking along a field edge path with a bank sloping down on the right to sea level. There is a wide area of salt marsh on the right.

At some houses by the shore, turn left for a few yards and then go right at a sign, passing in front of the dwellings. At the cart track go right for a few yards to continue left along the signed footpath and soon you are again by the river.

10. Gradually climb up the path. The path eventually comes to the end of Stourside, a cul-de-sac. Walk along the verge, beside bushes on the right. Opposite a road junction to the left, take a narrow path away from the road. Soon the path starts downhill a little. On reaching a junction of paths, turn right and in 10 yards go down rough steps to the shore. Turn left and follow the path beside the river back to the start.

PLACES OF INTEREST NEARBY

A prominent landmark is the tall mast which still stands at the former HMS *Ganges*, a shore-based boys' training establishment, which operated here from 1905 to 1976. The *HMS Ganges Museum* at the marina is open from April to October on weekends and bank holidays from 11 am to 5 pm. Telephone: 01473 684749 or 787291. A ferry runs from the Shotley Marina to the interesting Essex town of *Harwich*. For current details telephone: 0589 371138.

WALK 5

NEEDHAM MARKET LAKE AND THE RIVER GIPPING

This leisurely short walk starts beside Needham Market Lake, which once was gravel workings but has since been developed for recreational use – look out for wildlife here. Leaving the lake, the route continues more-or-less parallel to the River Gipping through the edge of the village to Hawks Mill, and then through new woodland and along a flowery meadow path to cross the river at Raven's Farm. The return is along part of the Gipping Valley Path.

The River Gipping

The graceful town of Needham Market lies in the shallow Gipping Valley. The River Gipping flows down to Ipswich where as the River Orwell it continues to the sea at Felixstowe. The terrain here is arable farmland with the river meandering through.

There are several pubs in Needham Market, among them the Swan in the High Street. This was built in the mid 16th century and in

1839 was a coaching inn. It has a large and pleasant bar. The varied menu includes bacon and onion suet pudding, various pasta dishes and vegetarian fare. Telephone: 01449 720280. There is also a coffee shop in the village.

- **HOW TO GET THERE:** Leave the A14 at the slip road for the A140 intersection and from the roundabout take the B1078 towards Needham Market. Shortly after crossing the river, you will see the lake on the right.
- **PARKING:** On the B1078, 300 yards from the river bridge and just before the railway bridge, there is a car park beside the lake.
- **LENGTH OF THE WALK:** 2½ miles. Maps: OS Landranger sheet 155 Bury St Edmunds and Sudbury area; Pathfinder 1007 Stowmarket and Coddenham (GR 094546).

THE WALK

1. From the warden's office block, go north on a gravel path following the edge of the lake. Where the gravel track goes right keep straight on, on a grassy path parallel to the railway on your left. Then pass Needham Market station on your left. Keep ahead with a playing field on your right.

Later, curving a little to the right, pass the wooden Scouts Headquarters building and some houses on the right. Pass through the pedestrian gate beside the wide metal gate. Continue on a wide tarmac track beside brick and flint walls on the right. Pass, on the left, Crown Cottages, built in 1869 and resembling a church.

2. Ignore the black metal pedestrian bridge on your right. You will pass the other end of this on the return journey. Continue round to the left, in Crown Street. Pass under the railway. Ahead you can see the High Street. Immediately after the bridge turn right up Constitution Hill. The road bends left and becomes King William Street.

3. At a T-junction turn right, and right again into Hawks Mill Street at the next T-junction. Where the road dives downward, keep up in front of a short row of houses to descend the steps at the end, and go under the railway bridge.

4. Soon you will come to a newish brick arch bridge over the river.

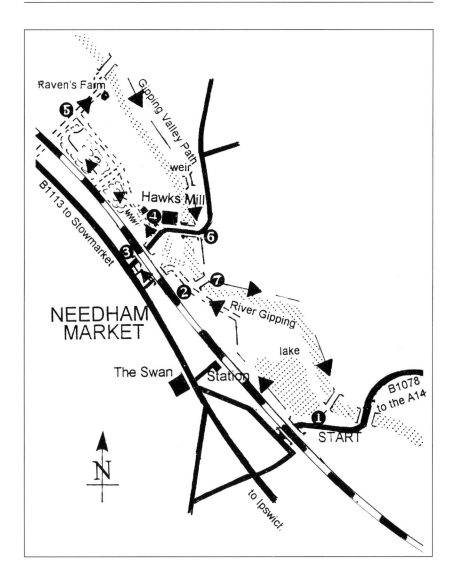

Ahead is impressive Hawks Mill. Next to the mill is fine double-fronted Hawks Mill House. Turn left before the bridge and walk with a watercourse on your right. Presently the track swings right, but you keep straight on, passing the end of a black weather-boarded cottage, and then some stables on the right. Continue on a wide path with a ditch on your left.

Leave the track and cross a stile where you are invited into newly created woodland. Alders, some oak, some ash and willow have been planted here. Walk a wide grass path through the young wood. Halfway along, cross a stile at each side of a footpath leading to steps up the railway embankment on the left. Go through the next stand of woodland, still on a broad grassy sward. Towards the end of the wood, the path sweeps right and left to a stile, where you rejoin the right of way.

The meadow opposite the new woodland is a flower-rich hay meadow which, as the notice tells, you are free to enjoy, going over to the river's edge if you wish.

5. From the stile turn left for 20 yards and turn right along a cart track which runs from a railway crossing on the left to Raven's Farm beside the river. After passing Raven's Farm on the right, keep beside the boarded fence and curve to the left. Turn right and cross a black steel girder footbridge to turn right along the Gipping Valley Path, following the east bank of the river. Come to an overflow weir, where floodwater can discharge down over some steps. Cross the weir by a bridge. A further 200 yards along, the path brings you to Hawks Mill Sluice and a timber footbridge.

6. Drop down and walk beside the river, under the concrete bridge. Continue along a grass path but soon join a surfaced footpath which has come from Alder Carr Farm at the edge of Creeting St Mary.

7. The path leads to the footbridge over the river which was passed earlier in the walk. Do not cross it but go over a one-step stile and continue along the grassy Gipping Valley Path, a well-used 18 mile long riverside path between Ipswich and Stowmarket.

Eventually, after passing a high security fence on the left, come to a laminated timber footbridge across the River Gipping leading directly back to the lake and the start.

PLACES OF INTEREST NEARBY

The area around the lake is a pleasant place to picnic and there are benches and tables at many points. On boards by the warden's office details are recorded of birds which have been seen recently.

THE RIVER GIPPING AT BRAMFORD

Follow the tranquil River Gipping downstream on this pleasant woodland walk from Bramford Meadows. Wildflowers grow in abundant profusion in Hazel Wood, particularly in the spring. After passing through Sproughton, the return is across farmland along the edge of the Gipping Valley.

The River Gipping at Bramford

Before the development of railways, the River Gipping provided a waterway to Stowmarket. Boats no longer use the river but the remains of many locks can still be seen. On the west side of the river, the land rises gently for about 100 feet and large fields growing cereals, rape or sugar beet are common along here.

The Wild Man, a well-appointed and popular pub, at the crossroads in Sproughton, would make a good refreshment stop on this walk. Its Carvery serves roast joints and there is also an excellent range of other dishes on offer. Telephone: 01473 724102.

- **HOW TO GET THERE:** The village of Bramford is just west of Ipswich. Exit the A14 at the B1113 (Great Blakenham) interchange, north of Ipswich. Follow the B1113 and in 2 miles bear left into Bramford, and after a left turn in the centre of the village, reach the river bridge. The start is at the picnic site just beyond the bridge.
- **PARKING:** Bramford picnic site. The access is opposite the John Keeble Garage.
- **LENGTH OF THE WALK:** 4 miles. Maps: OS Landranger sheet 169 Ipswich and The Naze area; Pathfinder 1030 Ipswich and Hadleigh. (GR 128465).

THE WALK

1. From the picnic site car park, cross the meadow to reach the river bank. Turn left beside the River Gipping and follow it downstream.

2. Cross several footbridges and soon reach the end of the meadow. Here climb a short flight of steps up into Hazel Wood, and go along a pleasant permissive path through the wood.

At the end the path swings right, back to the river bank. Turn left and continue along the Gipping Valley Path. Before long the bank is lined on both sides with tall mature trees. As you approach Sproughton, go through a narrow belt of woodland, to reach the remains of Sproughton Lock which now incorporates a sluice gate to control the water level in the river.

3. Just beyond the lock, cross a long bridge over a backwater and continue beside the river, and very soon climb steps up to the road and turn right over the river. Look right to see the old Sproughton Mill, now almost derelict. Walk straight up Lower West Street, passing a large black weatherboarded barn on the right. At the junction with the B1113 you come to a small green on the right.

4. Opposite is the Wild Man pub. Cross straight over the road and walk up Burstall Lane, passing the flank of the Wild Man and, a little further, Ransome Close on the left. Climb the hill for about 1/4 mile.

5. Just before the top of the rise, turn right at a footpath sign, climb the bank and continue across a field. From here is a good view of the Gipping Valley on the right.

After passing the end of a small wood on the left descend along a

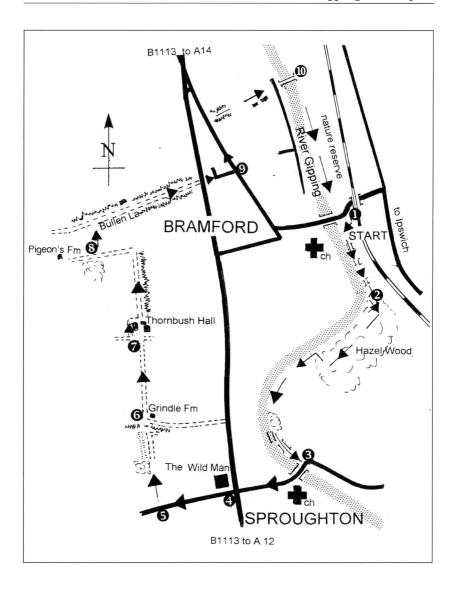

cart track. At the far side of the field, leave the cart track which turns right, bear slightly left and almost immediately drop down through a hedge to cross a small stream on a sleeper bridge. Climb a steep bank on the other side of the stream and go straight on through a newly planted plantation towards some light coloured cottages.

6. On reaching a lane leading off to the right, go half left along a wide grassy path for a few yards. At the corner of the plantation go straight on along a gravel farm road, towards Thornbush Hall.

7. At the corner of the farm buildings of Thornbush Hall, swing slightly left and continue beside a Dutch barn and then turn right, still following the gravel track. Under a radio mast turn left, walking beside a hedge on the right up the hill where you may see, on the right, the spire of Bramford church. Just beyond the top of the hill turn left, keeping along the farm track for about 100 yards.

8. At the corner of a new plantation on the left, turn right along a well-maintained grass path. On the far side of the field meet a road, Bullen Lane, and go right. Pass modernised Keepers Cottage on the left. Reach a road, cross straight over and take the tarmac path which leads into the head of a cul-de-sac, and go straight on.

9. At the T-junction turn left, passing the Methodist church on the right. Pass Acton Road on the right, and in 50 yards turn right along a narrow, signed footpath which leads past the entrance to a playing field on the left, and then past some dwellings down to a road beside the River Gipping.

10. Cross the road and then go over the Gipping footbridge. Turn right and continue beside the river. The riverside path takes you past the remains of the Bramford Lock which has a weir beside it. Climb a path up to the road, beyond which is the picnic site and the start. However, take a short diversion and cross the river bridge and look at Church Green, the first road on the left, leading to the church of St Mary the Virgin, where there are some fine looking houses.

PLACES OF INTEREST NEARBY
The centre of *Ipswich* is only 2 miles away. Why not stroll along the quay of the wet dock to pass the imposing frontage of the *Customs House*. *Christchurch Park* extends right to the edge of the shopping area and standing within it is *Christchurch Mansion,* a museum and art gallery. The *Ipswich Museum* is in High Street.

THE RIVER ORWELL AT FRESTON

Beginning in the shadow of Orwell Bridge, this walk takes us through leafy woodland to the village of Freston, with an optional detour to visit the dramatic 16th-century Freston Tower. The route continues to Wherstead where it follows field paths to the marina at Bourne Bridge. The return leg is along the river bank.

Orwell Bridge

Ipswich stands at the head of the Orwell Estuary. From the original dock area, close to the town centre, the Port of Ipswich extends southwards along both banks of the Orwell. Just beyond Cliff Quay, the graceful Orwell Bridge carries the Ipswich Bypass high over the river. Downstream, the River Orwell is part of an Area of Outstanding Natural Beauty (AONB). On higher ground above the Orwell estuary are Freston and Wherstead, both visited on this walk.

A little way into the route you come to the Freston Boot, a small, popular pub serving a good range of meals (telephone: 01473 780277). Later, almost opposite Bourne Bridge, you will find the

Oyster Reach pub and restaurant. Choices on the menu here include several traditional dishes such as Lancashire hot pot and beef stew and dumplings (telephone: 01473 692327).

- **HOW TO GET THERE:** Leave the A14, the Ipswich Bypass, at the A137 (Wherstead) interchange. Follow the A137 towards Ipswich and at the roundabout at the bottom of the hill, turn right on the B1456. Go under the Orwell Bridge and in $1/_4$ mile reach a layby on the left.
- **PARKING:** There are two laybys beside the shore on the B1456. If these are full there is a larger unsurfaced layby on the left $1/_2$ mile further on, just as the road climbs away from the river (at point 2).
- **LENGTH OF THE WALK:** $4^1/_2$ miles with an optional extra $1^1/_4$ miles to see Freston Tower. Maps: OS Landranger sheet 169 Ipswich and The Naze area; Pathfinder 1030 Ipswich and Hadleigh and 1053 Manningtree and Dedham (GR 170410).

THE WALK

1. From the Orwell Bridge walk beside the river at the edge of the road. Just as the road leaves the shore, bearing right and starting to climb Freston Hill, reach the unsurfaced layby.

2. Cross the road here and go through a wide gap in a fence and then take a path across the field. Make towards the wood on the far side of the field. Cross a stile under an old oak and then continue beside a hedge and in 100 yards enter Freston Wood by a stile. At a fork in the path keep right. The narrow path weaves through the wood of ash, sycamore, oak and sweet chestnut. Wildflowers abound here particularly in the spring. The path leaves the wood at a narrow road opposite Freston church.

For anyone who wishes to extend the walk to include Freston Tower, turn left along the road to the Freston Boot. Cross the Ipswich to Shotley road (Point 9 on map). Go 30 yards away from Ipswich and take the path signed to Wolverstone and Pin Mill. Drop down into a little valley and at the bottom come to a field. Follow a headland path with a fence on the left, up out of the valley.

At the corner of the field (Point 10 on map), turn left along a cart track signed to Freston Park. Before long cross a cattle grid and, leaving the track, bear half left towards the corner of a timber fence enclosing the garden of a large house. Go round to the left of the

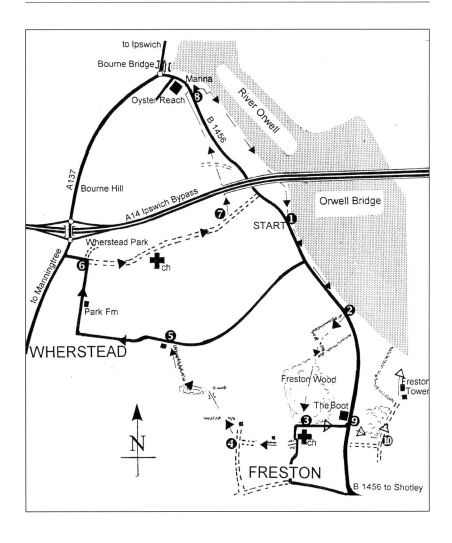

tower and walk straight down to the shore. There is no right of way along the shore and it is necessary to retrace your steps back to the road.

3. To continue the circular walk, turn right along the road and immediately follow the road round to the left. After passing a lychgate on the left and soon after a white bungalow on the right, the road starts to bend to the left. Here at a waymark swing right along a gravel drive between hedges.

At a Y-junction keep left as waymarked. Pass a cottage on the right, keeping straight on along a grass path which joins a wider track from the right. Continue through a wood to join a surfaced farm road.

4. Come to a T-junction, with a pair of houses at the corner. Leave the road and go straight on over a stile beside a tall holly bush, into a pasture. From the stile, go half right to a gate in the opposite side of the field. Continue in the same direction towards the valley bottom. Leave the field over two stiles.

Keep on in the same direction across the next meadow to a gap on the far side which is closed by two horizontal poles across the path; these can be untied and slid sideways, climbed over, or climbed through.

In about 20 yards, having walked through a tree belt, swing left beside a poplar plantation. At the end of the trees turn right along the headland with a hedge on the right and follow the cart track out to the road beside Redgate House. Turn left.

5. The next ³/₄ mile is along Vicarage Lane. After several gradual bends, the road makes a sharp right turn. Walk on along the road, passing, on the right, the black weatherboarded barn of Park Farm, and continue for ¹/₄ mile.

6. Where the road turns sharp left, turn right along a concrete path towards the church and the River Orwell.

After reaching Wherstead church, continue downhill. Soon you will have a fine panoramic view of the river. Pass, on the left, a brick cottage opposite two Dutch barns and, shortly after, pass a large cattle shed on the right.

7. About 100 yards beyond, turn left at a footpath sign towards the first bridge pier and the toe of the highway embankment. Cross a stile and walk under the bridge beside a fence on the left. Look up and you will be able to see that the Orwell Bridge was built as two, with a narrow gap between the two carriageways.

Go straight on at the end of the fence, and soon a stile will be visible a little to the left. Ahead lies Ipswich, and the cranes and quays of the port. After the stile cross a concrete access road and continue straight on towards the rear of houses. At the opposite side of the field continue, at first beside a clipped hedge on the right and then follow the edge of the field for $1/4$ mile with the rear gardens of a row of houses on the right. Near the corner of the field and before a large cream building, being the Oyster Reach pub, swing right and go through a narrow gap out to the road.

8. Cross the road and take a narrow, signed path opposite. The path lies beside the access way to Fox's Marina, and in 50 yards comes out into the marina by the Harbour Master's Office. Go a few yards along a concrete road, passing boat storage bays. Look out for a footpath sign opposite a workshop building on the right, and turn left for 10 yards beside a small grey portacabin to reach the edge of the Orwell Estuary. Turn right along a narrow path between the river and the boatyard.

The path continues on a well-walked path beside the river. On the opposite side of the river are quays where, several years ago, ships would discharge cargoes of coal to feed the former Cliff Quay Generating Station which has now been demolished.

Continue downstream and again walk under the Orwell Bridge. The deep water channel down the estuary lies between the green conical buoys and the red cylindrical (can) buoys. About 200 yards beyond the bridge the path comes to the road beside the first layby and the start of the walk.

PLACES OF INTEREST NEARBY

Just a few miles south is the picturesque riverside village of *Pin Mill.* There is a car park and picnic area here. Adjacent is *Cliff Plantation,* a 17 acre cliff top wood overlooking the Orwell, bought by the National Trust in 1979.

WALK 8

TRIMLEY MARSHES

There are plenty of opportunities for bird-spotting on this walk, which descends gradually from Trimley St Mary to the point where the River Orwell meets the River Stour. It then follows the river wall to Loompit Lake, a riverside expanse of water, where duck and wading birds often gather. The return is through farmland overlooking the river.

The River Orwell

The River Orwell is a busy waterway used by ships bound to and from the port of Ipswich and also by sailing boats and powered craft. Trimley Marshes lie on the east side of the Orwell, close to Felixstowe Docks. The area is crossed by many drainage ditches and is now given mainly to growing crops. From the flat, low lying fields the land rises to a plateau, where stand the twin villages of Trimley St Mary and Trimley St Martin.

The Hand in Hand pub at the northern end of Trimley St Martin and just a little way off the walk route, is a pleasant and comfortable establishment. The menu offers a good range of dishes, for example, pork loin chops, mixed grill, Suffolk smokie (flakes of smoked haddock in a rich sauce) and vegetarian options like leek, cheese and horseradish bake. Telephone: 01394 275249.

- **HOW TO GET THERE:** Follow the A14 road towards Felixstowe, and exit at the grade separated junction for Trimley Villages and Kirton. In $1/4$ mile go left at a roundabout and in $3/4$ mile turn right along Station Road. Cross the railway and continue to the end of the road.
- **PARKING:** There is a small car park at the end of Station Road, near the entrance to Searson's Farm.
- **LENGTH OF THE WALK:** 5½ miles. Maps: OS Landranger sheet 169 Ipswich and The Naze area; Pathfinder 1054 Felixstowe and Harwich (GR 278357).

THE WALK

1. From the car park at Searson's Farm go along the broad farm track in an avenue of oaks. In the distance, the massive cranes of Felixstowe Docks can be seen.

Along the track, pass two narrow bands of young trees. Later the path runs slightly downhill through mature woodland.

2. Turn right just by the corner of a tall earth bank and follow a wide hardcore track. Go through a gate at the entrance to the nature reserve and continue, between banks of newly planted screening, along the path which swings left round in a gentle curve towards the river.

On approaching the river wall, it is worth while to divert 100 yards to observe the birds from the Woodgate Hide.

3. Climb the river wall and turn right. The river, almost ½ mile wide at high tide, is on your left and, over to the right, the lakes which form part of the nature reserve can be seen. The river wall is a high grassy bank of soil forming a barrier to the low-lying marshes being flooded by the sea. The seaward side of the wall is strengthened in vulnerable places by stone and other hard material.

Pass, on the right, a hut belonging to the Suffolk Wildlife Trust and, spaced along the side of the reserve are three more hides. Instead of walking along the top of the river wall, you can drop down and go along the bridleway. To avoid being silhouetted on

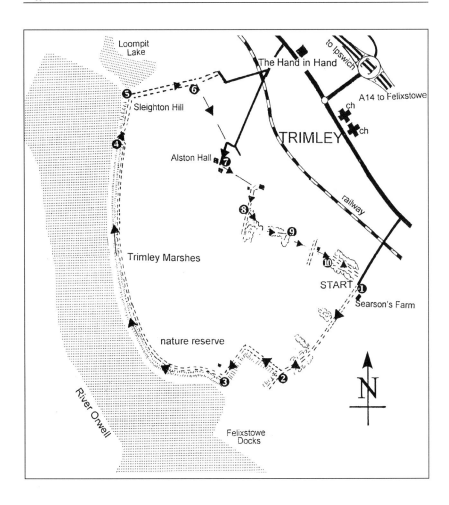

top of the wall it is a good idea to walk hidden below the bank and climb up and look over the wall from time to time to observe wading birds on the estuary.

At the time of writing there are proposals to open up the river wall to allow an area of marshland to be flooded. If this happens, the footpath will be diverted round the flooded marsh.

4. After 2 miles, the river wall merges into the side of a small hill and meets a broad track. Bear left along it, climbing Sleighton Hill. A wooded slope on the left drops steeply to the river.

Soon the lane descends almost to river level. Ahead is Loompit

Lake, a place for angling, and at this point the river bends left towards Pin Mill and Ipswich.

5. Turn right on a cart track and climb gradually. Near the top the track is crossed by electricity wires on wooden poles and, on the right, there is a newly planted tree belt.

6. Cross a makeshift stile beside a gate, then in 10 yards turn right along a track between fir trees. The conifer avenue comes out to a narrow road at a right-angle bend just by a white cottage. Swing right along the road towards the distant towering cranes.

7. The road ends at Alston Hall. Turn left immediately before a barn, and follow a grassy path between rows of newly planted trees, leading to a small shed. A field away is Grimston Hall. At the shed turn right along a cart track, as waymarked.

8. On reaching a small wood on the left, leave the cart track, bearing left through the wood on a narrow grassy path. Curve round to the left and skirt a small lake, turning right beyond it.

In 50 yards go left on a well-used path between rows of mixed trees. At the top of a short rise pause on a pleasantly located seat.

9. At the corner of the tree belt, turn right and continue for 100 yards through more trees and turn left. The path crosses a track at right angles. Keep straight on, passing an isolated pink house.

10. Where a footpath is signed to the right, go straight on and join Keeper's Track, with a hedge on the left and conifers and other trees forming a windbreak on both sides. The track leads through a gate and in 50 yards you come to Cordy's Lane. Turn right and walk back to the start.

PLACES OF INTEREST NEARBY

Ipswich Transport Museum in Cobham Road, on the south east side of Ipswich. Follow the A1156 towards Ipswich town centre and go sharp left at the first traffic signalled junction. Exhibits include buses, lorries, fire engines and bicycles. Open Sundays and bank holidays between April and October from 11 am to 5 pm; also Mondays to Fridays in August from 12 noon to 4 pm. Telephone: 01473 715666.

WALK 9
LANDGUARD POINT, FELIXSTOWE

This fascinating short walk around Landguard Point, unlike other walks in the book, is not on public rights of way but through a nature reserve to which members of the public are invited. The route takes you beside the sea to the jetty at the tip of the Point and then up to Landguard Fort and the specially constructed viewing area which overlooks Felixstowe Docks and from where you can see the massive container handling equipment.

Felixstowe beach

Felixstowe is a seaside town. However, it is now better known as one of Britain's busiest container ports.

The Rivers Orwell and Stour join and flow out to the sea at Felixstowe. The action of wind, tide and river flow has produced a great shingle promontory stretching seaward at the mouth of the rivers, called Landguard Point. As its name suggests, this area has been important for defence. Even in the 16th century Landguard Fort was positioned to control the access to the rivers and hence the way to the heart of Essex and Suffolk. Recently much of the area of the spit has been made a nature reserve.

As for refreshment, I would suggest visiting one of the many restaurants, cafés and bars in Felixstowe. The Regal Fish Restaurant, for example, is a pleasant, well-established place built in 1929 and conveniently situated on Sea Road at the southern end of Felixstowe not far from the fun fair. Telephone: 01394 282678.

- **HOW TO GET THERE:** Follow the A14 main road to Felixstowe. At the large roundabout at the edge of the town go right, signed 'A14 Felixstowe Docks'. At the next roundabout go straight on, signed 'Town Centre'. Turn right at the traffic signals and in $1/4$ mile, where the main road bends right, go straight on and turn left. Later turn right along Manor Terrace to the car park at the end.
- **PARKING:** Suffolk Coastal District Council's Manor Terrace car park (free; maximum stay 18 hours). There are public toilets here.
- **LENGTH OF THE WALK:** 2 miles. Maps: OS Landranger sheet 169 Ipswich and The Naze area; Pathfinder 1054 Felixstowe and Harwich (GR 290326).

THE WALK

Note: Access to certain areas of the nature reserve may be restricted from time to time and visitors are asked to comply with all notices.

1. Leave Manor Terrace car park by a pedestrian exit close to an information board about the nature reserve, and follow a gravel path to climb an embankment from which can be seen a wide expanse of the coastline. Keep to the top of the embankment but in 200 yards drop down some steps and then climb up to walk along a similar embankment running parallel to the sea wall on the left. On the right is the southern end of Felixstowe Docks. Behind the quays are the extensive container handling and storage areas.

2. Eventually leave the bank and enter, through a pedestrian gap in a steel barrier, the Suffolk Wildlife Trust's nature reserve, and continue along a concrete track, still parallel to the beach.

3. In nearly 300 yards, the track is joined by a concrete roadway on the right coming from Landguard Fort, the car parks and the Docks viewing area. The walk returns here later.

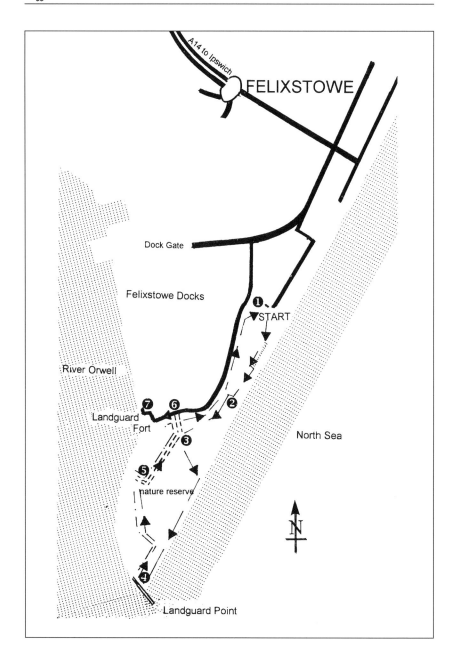

Continue along the concrete but soon make your way across the open ground to the coastline.

Walk southward beside the sea, skirting, where necessary, areas fenced to prevent disturbance to ground-nesting birds.

4. Keep along the beach to the derelict jetty at the tip of Landguard Point. Here you can see the wide sweep of coast from Walton-on-the-Naze to the whole of Felixstowe beach.

Turn round and retrace your steps, keeping beside the tall chainlink fence. At the corner of the fence follow it round to the left, passing old concrete anti-tank blocks.

Cross a concrete track leading to a gate on the left and, still beside the fence, reach an isolated red brick dwelling on the left. Turn half right along another track which leads to the corner of the site.

5. Turn away from the water, along a well-used track. On the left, behind a high fence is the Bird Observatory.

Keep along the concrete track and at the junction where you were earlier, swing round to the left beside the Bird Observatory fence and leave the nature reserve by a kissing gate.

6. Passing Landguard Fort, turn left along the narrow road to the Felixstowe Docks viewing area.

At the time of writing, a new ferry service runs from here. A small craft with a ramp at its bow beaches on the shingle and takes passengers across the harbour to Harwich and thence to Shotley.

7. Retrace your steps back to the nature reserve and go through the kissing gate. About 10 yards beyond the gate, turn left along a narrow path climbing the embankment. At the top pass some concrete Second World War defence structures. Where the path divides keep slightly left but continue close to the top of the rampart. Descend steps to the barrier and follow the gravel path towards a caravan site in the distance. About 100 yards before reaching the end of the Reserve turn right back to the car park and the start.

PLACES OF INTEREST NEARBY

Landguard Fort (English Heritage) is open on Sundays and public holidays from early May to the end of September (mainly guided tours, 10.30 am to 4.30 pm), also on Wednesdays from mid June to the end of August (2 pm to 5 pm). Telephone: 01394 277767.

FALKENHAM, THE RIVER DEBEN AND KING'S FLEET

Some splendid wide views can be enjoyed on this walk, which visits Falkenham church and then descends to cross lonely marshes to the River Deben opposite Ramsholt. The return is beside King's Fleet, a broad river which drains the marshes. For a longer walk, you can continue beside the Deben to its mouth at the isolated settlement of Felixstowe Ferry.

Felixstowe Ferry

Although only 3 miles north of Felixstowe, Falkenham is a tiny village on slightly higher ground overlooking the River Deben.

Three miles away at Newbourne just north of Kirton, is the Fox inn. This is a popular, comfortable pub with oak beams and settles, and a warming fire on cold days. The changing menu provides a good choice of fare, such as game pie, the Fox brunch (sausage, bacon, egg, black pudding and chips), and beef stew and dumplings. Telephone: 01473 736307. At the hamlet of Felixstowe Ferry, reached on the longer walk, there are two possibilities for refreshment. The Ferry Café serves fish and chips, various omelettes and a range of other snacks. Telephone: 01394 276305. Nearby is the Ferry Boat Inn offering a range of good food. Telephone: 01394 284203.

- **HOW TO GET THERE:** Leave the A14 just north of Felixstowe at the grade separated interchange for Trimley Villages and Kirton. Take the exit signed 'Kirton'. In 200 yards turn sharp right, beside the Trimley picnic area, along Capel Hall Lane, towards Falkenham. In $1/2$ mile, turn left for a further $1/2$ mile and at the T-junction go right. Keep straight on to the end of the public road at Deben Lodge Farm.
- **PARKING:** Park on a verge immediately in front of a bungalow, Deben View, where there are a few parking spaces – there is a sign saying 'Public Parking'. In the unlikely event that the spaces are all occupied, the only other parking option is at the Trimley picnic area.
- **LENGTH OF THE WALK:** 5 miles or 7 miles if you extend the walk to Felixstowe Ferry. Maps: OS Landranger sheet 169 Ipswich and The Naze area; Pathfinder 1054 Felixstowe and Harwich (GR 300382)

THE WALK

1. From the parking area outside Deben View, walk back along the road and turn right at the first junction. Enter Falkenham and after passing Russell's Farm on the left, come to Sheepgate Lane, leading to Goseford Hall, on the right.

2. Opposite Sheepgate Lane go half left on a signed cross-field path. At the field corner, drop down a steep bank, out to the road. Swing left and in 20 yards, turn right along a gravel farm road. In a few yards pass the gate to Falkenham church on the left.

3. On reaching a junction of tracks, turn right on a grassy-middled cart track beside a hedge on the right. Enjoy the fine panoramic view of the River Deben. At the end of the field descend a lane on the left with hedges on both sides. Bear right at the bottom, still following the lane.

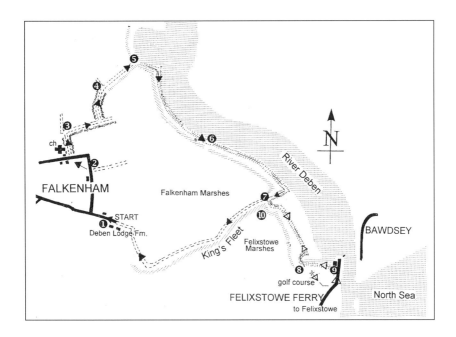

4. In ¹/₄ mile, at a junction, keep half right along a grass path beside a ditch. On a hill in the distance you can see Ramsholt church.

5. After crossing a broad ditch, the path ends at the foot of the river wall. Climb the bank. Ahead you will see Falkenham Creek and beyond it, on the opposite bank, the Ramsholt Arms pub. The route continues to the right along the top of the river wall. A broad drainage channel runs parallel to the river and there is a grassy margin between it and the river wall. For anyone interested in seeing duck, geese and other wading birds, it is a good idea to walk hidden below the bank, and from time to time climb the bank and look over to the river and the mud-flats.

6. Eventually you come to a point where there is a sluice and an outfall through the river wall. A sign indicates a path away from the river, but keep straight on beside the estuary.

On the opposite side of the river is a tall radio mast and almost opposite the mast, the river wall makes a sharp turn to the right round a small creek into which King's Fleet discharges. In 150 yards reach the head of the creek at a three-way footpath sign.

7. From this point the 5 mile walk descends the river wall and continues away from the Deben Estuary along a cinder track beside King's Fleet (see point 10 below).

For those who have the time, a visit to the mouth of the Deben at Felixstowe Ferry is recommended. For the longer walk keep on the river wall round the head of the creek and shortly cross a stile. In under ½ mile the bank turns sharp right again round another small creek, at the head of which go over a stile and stride over the top of steel flood protection piling.

8. Drop down off the top of the river wall, swing left along the toe of the bank for 50 yards and then, turning right, make your way to a waymark. Cross the golf course to a bridge over a wide ditch and continue along a gravel track. Pass Tee 5 and swing right to take a narrow footpath across some rough ground towards houses and the Ferry Boat Inn. The path leads out between houses to the road.

Turn left along the road to the landing stage, from where a ferry service operates across the river to Bawdsey. Nearby is the Ferry Café. Explore the shingle beach at the mouth of the river.

9. Return along the road and 50 yards beyond the Ferry Café, turn right, along a surfaced footpath beside a low steel flood protection wall. This is not a definitive right of way but is used by the public. Continue along the river wall back to the three-way sign you passed earlier at the mouth of King's Fleet.

10. Where the river wall makes a sharp turn, drop steeply off the river wall. Cross a stile and join a cinder cart track running parallel to King's Fleet, 100 yards away, on the left. Continue along the track for about a mile and then follow the track gradually round to the right. After a slight bend left, you pass white painted Deben Lodge on the left, and soon after return to Deben View and the start.

PLACES OF INTEREST NEARBY
Newbourne Springs Nature Reserve is 3 miles north of Falkenham. Situated in a small wooded valley it is managed by the Suffolk Wildlife Trust. There is a Visitors' Centre and a circular walk (GR 273433).

MARTLESHAM CREEK

This pleasant short stroll from Martlesham church goes down to the bank of the River Deben where you can wander southwards for a little way to see the tranquil river scenery. The quay at Woodbridge can be seen a mile upstream and 2 miles away, on a hill overlooking Woodbridge, is the site where the Sutton Hoo Burial Ship was excavated. Return along the southern side of Martlesham Creek, enjoying fine views of the estuary.

The River Deben

Martlesham Heath is a newly developed village beside the A12 Ipswich Bypass. Martlesham, the original village, is about a mile away, close to the head of Martlesham Creek, a quiet tidal inlet off the River Deben. As with all the wide river estuaries of Suffolk, this is an important boating area. Boats can sail up the creek to the boatyard just below Martlesham church, but the main centres are Waldringfield, downstream, and Woodbridge a mile or so upstream. However, the creek and the surrounding countryside are very quiet and this is a good place to watch for duck and other wading birds.

The Red Lion in Martlesham village, just west of the walk route, is a well-appointed and popular pub. It serves excellent bar meals and also has a carvery. Telephone: 01394 382169.

- **HOW TO GET THERE:** From the roundabout on the A12 at the junction with the A1214 (the road to Ipswich), go east on a local road. In a mile turn right at the Red Lion public house along a minor road towards Waldringfield. In a further $1/2$ mile turn left towards Martlesham church on a no through road and at the end of the road swing right into the church car park.
- **PARKING:** St Mary's church car park. Visitors are invited to contribute towards upkeep by putting coins in a slot in the top of a small green steel container.
- **LENGTH OF THE WALK:** $2^1/_2$ miles but there is also the opportunity to explore further along the river wall. Maps: OS Landranger sheet 169 Ipswich and The Naze area; Pathfinder 1031 Woodbridge (GR 260469).

THE WALK

1. From the car park go down the hill, following the row of lime trees on the left. At the bottom of the hill, where the row of trees ends, go left at a three-way footpath sign, called Doughtys Way. Walk between the stable block on the right and a tall garden wall on the left. Just by the corner of Martlesham Hall, go right through a pedestrian gate and in a few yards go left along a cart track with a long narrow pond on the left.

Just beyond the pond, a path over the stile on the left leads directly to St Mary's church. Unless you wish to visit the church, continue straight on along a lane with hedges on both sides.

2. The lane comes out into the corner of a field by a three-way footpath sign, 'Smugglers' Run'. Keep straight on along a wide grassy headland path with a ditch on the right. Note a footpath which goes off to the right soon after. Keep straight on. You may still see, on the right, an old wooden board bearing the legend 'Kanga Bosk. Here sleeps a faithful companion and friend 1958–1968'.

3. The path goes half right at a corner and, at the side of the field, it crosses a culvert into a poplar plantation. It soon swings left to join

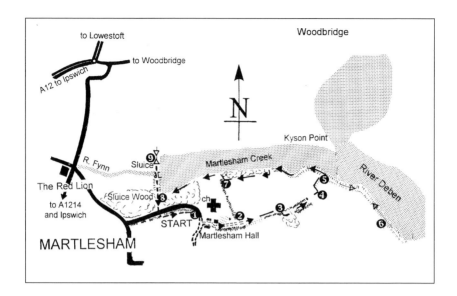

a track, which continues as a green lane between hedges. In about 100 yards, the lane swings left and right and continues between fences.

4. Cross a stile beside a gate into a pasture. Immediately turn left and walk beside a hedge on the left. After crossing a sleeper bridge go sharp right beside a ditch on the right. At the end of the field, cross a stile which leads to a bridge and then climb the river wall.

5. At this point you are at the end of Martlesham Creek, where it meets the Deben Estuary. Opposite is a promontory known as Kyson Point and, looking slightly right, you will see Woodbridge.

At one time, the path going right along the top of the river wall led to Waldringfield about a mile down the Deben Estuary. The river wall was breached in the 1950s. The present path is only a cul-de-sac but walking a little way along it to the right for about ¼ mile and back, gives good views of the river towards Waldringfield.

6. To continue the walk retrace your steps and then continue along the river wall, following Martlesham Creek on the right. Shortly the path veers left, leaving the river wall, to go through a narrow belt of trees to a large field. Turn right along a grassy headland path.

7. On getting to the corner of the field, turn right at a three-way footpath sign, back through the tree belt, towards the river. Cross a stile into a meadow with the creek, fringed with rushes, on the right. Keep to the edge of the field and at the corner go through a waymarked gap along a path through woods which leads over a stile into a boatyard. In about 200 yards, where the boatyard track swings right, keep straight on, as waymarked, along a narrow woodland path.

8. In 200 yards pass a stile and cross a two-plank bridge, to reach a well-used track at right angles. Here go right at first, passing another stile and, on leaving the wood, continue along the river wall, flanked with gorse bushes, to reach the head of Martlesham Creek.

9. The River Fynn drains through sluice gates into Martlesham Creek. Here you have a good view of the tidal creek to the right and the riverside meadow and marsh to the left. The path ahead leads to Woodbridge, $1^1/2$ miles away.

Retrace your steps, passing the path (off left) where you were earlier and continue straight on, climbing through the woods. At the top of the rise, cross a stile out to a road. Climb a shallow bank into the field opposite. Turn left and follow the hedge on the left, which leads back to the Martlesham church car park.

PLACES OF INTEREST NEARBY
Woodbridge is 2 miles away, at the head of the Deben Estuary. The town with its quay is a pleasant place and well worth a visit. In a prominent position beside the river is the 19th-century *Woodbridge Tide Mill*, now restored to working order. Open from May to September daily, 1 pm to 5 pm, and in October, weekends only. Telephone: 01473 626618. *Buttrum's Windmill*, also in Woodbridge, is open between May and September, Saturdays, Sundays and bank holidays, 2 pm to 6 pm. Telephone: 01473 583352. *Suffolk Horse Museum* in Market Hill, Woodbridge shows the history and development of the Suffolk Punch. Open Easter Monday to September daily 2 pm to 5 pm. Telephone: 01394 380643.

THE BUTLEY RIVER AND BOYTON MARSHES

Starting at the edge of Rendlesham Forest, and passing close to ancient Butley Priory, the walk continues along the Suffolk Coast and Heaths Path to Burrow Hill. From the crest of this tiny hill, there is a magnificent view of the coastal plain and the river estuaries. The route then follows the Butley River to the River Ore. The return is through the village of Boyton, across rolling farmland and alongside the forest. Take binoculars and a bird-book with you!

Looking south along Butley River

Much of this isolated and sparsely populated area is flat low-lying marsh, criss-crossed with drainage ditches, the home to many species of birds. Because of this, Boyton Marshes are an RSPB nature reserve. The Butley River is a short river discharging through a 3 mile long tidal estuary into the River Ore. Opposite the mouth of the Butley River, and lying in the River Ore, is Havergate Island, another RSPB bird reserve. Between the Ore and the sea is the huge shingle bank of Orford Spit.

Situated at a road junction on the B1084, a short drive north of the walk route, is the Butley Oyster Inn. It is said that this old inn was once the haunt of smugglers who brought their contraband up the Butley River. This pleasant establishment has a good range of food on offer. Telephone: 01394 450790.

- **HOW TO GET THERE:** From the roundabout on the A12, north east of Woodbridge, take the A1152 road towards Snape. A mile beyond Wilford Bridge over the River Deben, go straight on along the B1084 towards Orford. In about 3 miles, soon after Butley Corner picnic site, fork right along a minor road signed to 'Capel Green' and 'Butley Corner'. In about ½ mile come to a road junction to the right signed 'Capel St Andrew'. This is the start of the walk.
- **PARKING:** There is a wide verge beside the forest at the minor road junction at Capel Green.
- **LENGTH OF THE WALK:** 7 miles, or 5 miles if you choose to take the short cut from Boyton Dock, omitting Boyton Marshes. Maps: OS Landranger sheet 169 Ipswich and The Naze area for the walk; the B1084 and Butley village are shown on sheet 156 Saxmundham, Aldeburgh and surrounding area; Pathfinder 1031 Woodbridge (GR 368495).

THE WALK

1. From Capel Green road junction, go east along the road towards Butley High Corner. In ¼ mile look right to see the magnificent 14th century former gatehouse of Butley Priory. It is now a dwelling.

2. At the road junction turn right and in 50 yards go left along a wide green lane. The lane ends and the track continues beside a hedge on the right. At the end of the field, keep straight on and shortly come to a road at Butley High Corner and turn left. In 100 yards the road becomes a wide stony track ending at a T-junction.

3. Turn right along the Suffolk Coast and Heaths Path, denoted by its characteristic waymark. In 50 yards keep beside Bush Covert, a mixed wood, on the left. Beyond the wood, walk towards Burrow Hill along a wide grassy track between ditches 20 yards apart. Cross a stile beside twin gates and climb the hill. At the top you are

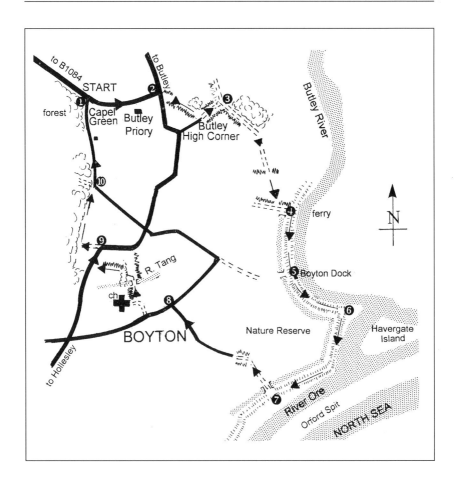

suddenly presented with a breathtaking view. Ahead is the Butley River, winding its way between coastal marshes to the River Ore in the distance, whilst beyond is Orford Spit and the North Sea. On the hill top there are some shallow excavations, the site of an archaeological dig some years ago when Bronze Age remains were found.

Cross a stile and descend through a pasture to another stile and then go left towards the river. Cross a stile and climb the river wall. Ahead is the landing stage for the Butley Ferry.

4. Turn right and continue, over several stiles, along the river wall for ¼ mile until you reach Boyton Dock, a riverside quay. Alongside it are the remains of an old brick barn, a remnant from the time when ships traded along the coast bringing supplies to the isolated villages.

5. At this point a path leads inland, so should you wish to make a direct return to the start, go 50 yards back along the bank and drop down to a squeezer stile and take the path away from the river. In due course the grass path gives way to a concrete track past some barns. Continue on to reach a road at a bend. Go straight on for just over ¹/₂ mile to a crossroads by Home Farm. Go straight over and in another ¹/₂ mile turn right at a bend to rejoin the longer walk (see point 10).

The full walk continues along the river wall. The Butley River is on the left, and beyond that, across the marshes, you can see Orford's castle, church and, further to the right, lighthouse. This is a quiet spot and as you look across saltings and marshes you may well spot interesting birds feeding at the river's edge. Being shy creatures they will soon fly off to a 'safe' distance away.

6. Reach, in ¼ mile, a point where the river wall makes a right-angled turn to the right. Here the Butley River joins the River Ore and directly ahead there is Havergate Island where avocets breed and, on the right, Boyton Marshes, a wide expanse of flat fields. The path makes another turn to the right at Flybury Point. Look left to see Dove Point, the southern tip of Havergate Island.

All the way from Boyton Dock there has been a drainage ditch running parallel to the river wall about 15 yards away. Notice the level of the water in the ditch compared with the level of the tidal river. Water in the drainage ditch is discharged to the sea at low tide or pumped out, if necessary, at other times.

About ¹/₂ mile from Flybury Point, look out for a ramp and a small track which crosses the saltings to a place where the boats from the village are pulled up. Opposite the ramp is a gap in the drainage ditch leading to a track across the field.

7. Turn right here and cross a stile to follow the track across the field. At the opposite side, the track bears leftish into a lane. In 200 yards, pass a turning left to Boyton Hall Farm. Keep straight on along the road to a T-junction at Boyton village street.

8. Turn left for ¼ mile, and then turn right along a lane, with hedges both sides, towards Boyton House. Where the main surfaced track bends left towards the house, fork right along a narrower surfaced track towards the stables. At the entrance to the stable yard, keep left across a stile and continue between a hedge on the left and a ranch-style fence on the right.

At the end of the fence enter a rough meadow, but do not follow a grass track which sweeps round to the right. Take a narrow, little-used path through the grass, parallel to the field boundary on the left, which leads to a stile and a narrow bridge over the River Tang. Come to an uncultivated end of a field. Go half left and cross the rough field to the wood. After crossing a ditch on a two-sleeper bridge, walk through the small oak wood to the field beyond, swing right and follow a grassy track beside the wood. Where the wood ends keep straight on across the field for about 50 yards and turn right along the road.

9. At the bend in the road turn sharp left along a sandy bridleway. On reaching the corner of a field turn right on a broad grass path with a replanted forest on the left.

10. Come out to a road at a right-angled bend. Keep straight on along this quiet road for ½ mile, passing Green Farm, back to Capel Green and the start.

PLACES OF INTEREST NEARBY
Forest Enterprises have a car park and Visitors' Centre at *Tangham* in Rendlesham Forest (GR 353484) with a nature trail and cycle hire facilities. Situated almost at the foot of Burrow Hill, the privately operated *Butley Ferry* plies across the Butley River giving access northward towards Orford. Anyone wishing to use the ferry should contact the ferryman, Bryan Rogers, on 01394 410096.

ORFORD AND THE RIVER ALDE

An ancient castle, a dramatic lighthouse, an interesting martello tower and a 10-mile long shingle spit are all to be seen on this exciting walk from Orford Quay – a long trek, but worth the effort!

Aldeburgh

Orford Ness is a great shingle bank, the largest in Europe, which stretches along the North Sea coast from Aldeburgh, southwards for 10 miles. This remote and isolated area is an important nature reserve, where rare plants flourish and where many bird species gather at varying seasons of the year.

Standing beside the River Alde is the picturesque village of Orford, with its castle. From the quay, a ferry runs across the river, here called the River Ore, to the National Trust property on the Ness.

The Old Warehouse Café and Restaurant is by the quay. It specialises in grilled and deep fried fish, from landings at the quay, and is open Wednesdays to Sundays. Telephone: 01394 450210. There are several refreshment options in Orford, including the

Crown and Castle, a pleasant hotel close to Orford Castle. Telephone: 01394 450205.

- **HOW TO GET THERE:** From a roundabout on the A12 just north of Woodbridge take the A1152 towards Snape. In about 2 miles keep straight on along the B1084 to Orford. Follow the signs to the quay.
- **PARKING:** A Pay and Display car park is on the left just before the quay.
- **LENGTH OF THE WALK:** 10 miles. There are no short cuts, but it is an attractive path beside the River Alde. If 10 miles is too far, why not go a few miles along the river wall and retrace your steps? Maps: OS Landranger sheet 156 Saxmundham, Aldeburgh and surrounding area, also a tiny part on 169 Ipswich and The Naze area; Pathfinder 1009 Aldeburgh and Orford (GR 425496).

THE WALK

1. From the car park turn left towards the quay. In a few yards, immediately before the Old Warehouse Restaurant, turn left along a narrow grass path. Soon pass a boatyard on the right and shortly after, a house on the left. Before long, you will be following a wide path along the top of a grassy bank which forms a flood protection wall between the tidal estuary and the low lying meadows to the left. The walk follows the top of the bank for 5 miles and there will be a number of stiles to cross en route.

On the way, see over to the right the red and white striped Orford Ness Lighthouse which is on the seaward edge of the Orford Spit. The spit is now a nature reserve but a number of the former research buildings can be seen. Further on you will pass, on the opposite side of the River Alde, a large shed-like building with an associated array of eleven tall radio masts.

2. Having got almost opposite the last aerial mast on the right, pause and look round behind you, to see Orford Ness Lighthouse, Orford Castle and the church tower.

On the left, almost all the way from Orford, there is a broad drainage channel running parallel to the river wall and crossed by occasional cart bridges. This is a common feature beside the tidal estuaries in Suffolk.

Eventually, about 5 miles from Orford, come to a point opposite the martello tower. This fortification, built in Napoleonic times, sits

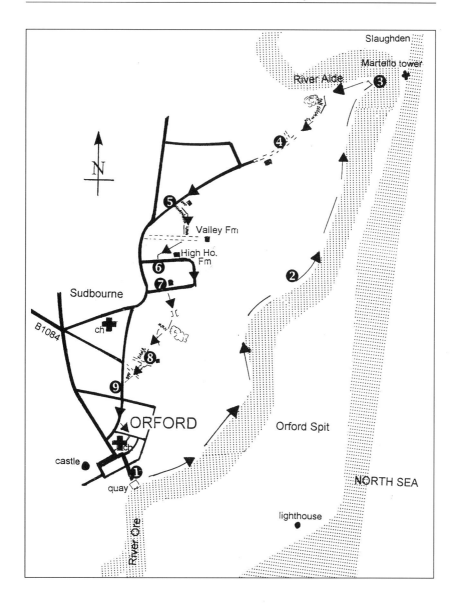

astride the narrow shingle bank which separates the River Alde from the sea and is the start of the large spit of shingle forming Orford Ness. A little beyond the martello tower is Slaughden Quay.

3. At this point the river makes a sharp bend to the left. Continue on the river wall and about ½ mile beyond the bend, and just before a plantation of conifers, go left at a three-way footpath sign over a stile next to an iron gate. Keep to the edge of the field and shortly bear right with a ditch on the right. After a small pond cross a stile beside a gate and follow a cart track. On the left pass an old stable and then continue along a concrete farm track.

4. At a T-junction of tracks bear leftish and before long the concrete track leads into a road. Pass through two pairs of white gates and continue along the surfaced road. Keep straight on at a T-junction. Pass a track off to the left and, shortly after, a wood on the right, where some of the oak trees look very old.

5. About 100 yards beyond Airey Cottages, a pair of dwellings, on the left, turn left along a sandy cart track. Leave the track where it swings right and go straight ahead over a stile beside a metal gate into a meadow and keep a fence and ditch on the right.

At a field boundary cross a wide cart bridge over a drainage channel and walk towards Valley Farm, a field away. About 100 yards before reaching a farm building, turn right over a stile into the field on the right. Immediately turn left and continue beside the fence, now on the left, to the end of the field. Cross straight over Valley Farm's sandy access road and, turning half right, take a path diagonally across the field.

At the field corner ignore an inviting stile into an orchard on the left but go generally in the same direction on a winding way through a tree belt. There should not be any stiles to cross on this part of the walk. Observe and follow waymarks and eventually come out to a path beside a plantation of young trees on the right. At the end of the plantation go through a steel gate, along a narrow path which leads to a road 50 yards away.

6. Turn left along the narrow road and pass wisteria-clad High House Farm. The road bends right and at the bottom of the hill you turn right and continue past Crag Farm on the right.

7. When you reach a wide gap in the hedge on the left turn left. Go through a red gate into a meadow and keep beside a ditch on the left. After crossing a timber bridge, bear half right towards the right hand edge of a wood about 200 yards away.

Just by the corner of the wood cross a two-sleeper bridge with handrails and skirt the wood on the left. Going through a gap at a field boundary turn half right to a stile in a wire fence. After the stile keep in the same direction across the field to a hedge 200 yards away, and then continue with the hedge on the right.

8. On reaching the end of the hedge, a waymark points straight on, but if the path ahead is not clear, turn left for 50 yards along a cart track towards a brick building and then turn right, following a wide grass path between hedges. At the end of the green lane come to a junction with a cart track at right angles leading to Lodge Farm. Move 5 yards to the right, and then turn left, through a gate, into a field.

Continue along a pleasant headland path with the hedge on the right. At the corner of the field, where the hedge turns right, keep straight on, parallel to the boundary on the right, making for a point 10 yards left of a double electricity pole. Go through a narrow gap, out to a road.

9. Turn left and in 200 yards keep straight on at the crossroads. At the 30 mph sign, go left along a footpath through a field which leads out between gardens to a road. Cross straight over and continue, beside a wall on the right, on a narrow path which leads to the churchyard. Follow the path round to the west end of the church, where a gate leads directly to Market Hill, which is worth seeing.

To return to the start at the quay, go through the south gate of the churchyard and continue straight along the road for 1/4 mile.

PLACES OF INTEREST NEARBY

On a small knoll close to Orford's Market Hill stands *Orford Castle*. This English Heritage castle, built in the reign of Henry II, is open daily between April and September from 10 am to 6 pm (or dusk) and during the rest of the year on Wednesdays to Sundays from 10 am to 4 pm. Telephone: 01604 730320. *Orford Ness* (National Trust) offers pedestrian trails, various displays and occasional guided walks. Generally open on Thursdays, Fridays and Saturdays. Access by boat from Orford Quay, which runs frequently between 10 am and 12.30 pm. For details and booking telephone: 01394 450057.

THE RIVER ALDE AND THE SEA AT ALDEBURGH

The low-lying fields and marshes along the edge of the Alde Estuary, which this walk follows, are a haven for birds. The route then crosses fields on the west of the town and continues along the former railway line towards Thorpeness. Later, the walk passes 16th-century Moot Hall, almost on the beach. By way of contrast, a few hundred yards beyond, is the new lifeboat station, a fine structure of modern design.

The River Alde

Aldeburgh is a quiet seaside town. Formerly it was a port of some significance but the coastal shipping trade declined and its harbour was silted up, and it ceased to be a port centuries ago.

A narrow band of shingle is all that prevents the River Alde discharging to the sea at Slaughden. However over centuries coastal material has been driven by wind and tidal currents to accumulate to form Orford Ness, and the River Alde is forced south at Slaughden to flow between the coastal marshes and the heap of shingle of The Ness for 10 miles to discharge to the sea at Shingle Street.

Just beyond Slaughden and at the edge of Orford Spit stands a large martello tower. Dating from the Napoleonic War, these old defensive structures which are dotted along the coast are usually circular. However, the one at the end of Orford Spit consists of four circles joined together rather like a four leafed clover. The building is owned by the Landmark Trust and viewing is by appointment with the housekeeper (telephone: 01728 453879).

There are several hotels, pubs, restaurants and cafés in Aldeburgh. Among them is the Captain's Cabin, a comfortable restaurant and tea room in High Street serving freshly prepared, home-cooked food. Telephone: 01728 452520.

- **HOW TO GET THERE:** From the A12 a few miles south of Saxmundham take the A1094 to Aldeburgh. Keep on through the town centre and eventually reach an unmade gravel road. Fork right, to the sailing area at Slaughden.
- **PARKING:** The Suffolk Coastal District Council's Slaughden Quay car park which is at the end of the gravel road.
- **LENGTH OF THE WALK:** 5½ miles, or 3½ miles if you choose to take the short cut, omitting the walk by the sea to the north of Aldeburgh. Maps: OS Landranger sheet 156 Saxmundham, Aldeburgh and surrounding area; Pathfinder 1009 Aldeburgh and Orford (GR 464555).

THE WALK

1. From the Slaughden Quay car park walk back 50 yards and take the gravel footpath on the left along the river wall with the River Alde and Slaughden Quay on the left. On the right of the river wall is a wide drainage ditch, parallel to the river. Beyond, on a small hill, stands the town of Aldeburgh.

Pass steps going down the bank on the right and continue along the bank beside the river. There are a number of stiles to cross along the route.

2. Continue along the river wall to West Row Point where the river makes a sharp bend to the right.

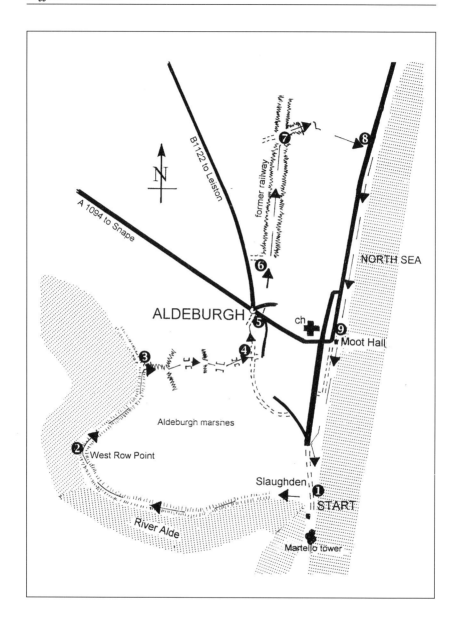

3. In about ¹/₂ mile, where the river bends left, leave the river wall, descending steps on the right. Continue away from the river beside a fence and hedge on the left. Pass a farm gate on the left and at a field corner cross a stile beside a gate into a meadow. Go over the field, bearing slightly left, towards a hurdle in the far fence. A large notice on a wooden electricity pole points the way.

Pass through the hurdle and cross a ditch. Walk across the next field in a direction a little to the right of the distant water tower on a hill. Negotiate a similar hurdle on the far side of the pasture and take a cross-field path which leads via a timber bridge to another meadow.

Keep straight on and reach yet another footbridge and, beyond it, a few yards of uncultivated ground, a two-plank bridge and an allotment garden. Go through the allotments and leave by a pedestrian gate leading to a wide path at right angles.

4. The path to the right leads back to the road to Slaughden. This is a short cut back to the start.

For the main walk, turn left between an old buttressed brick wall on the right and a clipped hedge on the left. Cross the recreation ground, pausing perhaps to rest on the seats beside the wall.

Beyond the sports ground, a short access track leads to the main road at a roundabout.

5. Turn right along the road for about 100 yards and then left along a narrow, unsurfaced footpath between a bungalow called Pathways and a newish brick wall on the left. In 100 yards obliquely cross an estate road to keep straight on along a narrow footpath. Come to a caravan site. There is a public footpath going right here, but keep straight on along the path which is within a strip of land with fences on both sides.

6. Eventually, see on the left the head of a cul-de-sac, and, opposite, on the right, a stile leading across a caravan site. Keep straight on along a permissive path, following the route of the former Leiston to Aldeburgh railway.

7. After about $1/4$ mile reach a public footpath crossing at right angles, and here turn right, leaving the former railway.

Having turned right, immediately cross a stile beside an iron gate, and continue on a broad path between fences. Look left to see Thorpeness Windmill and, behind it, the 'House In The Clouds', a dwelling incorporated in and disguising a water tower. Further left, is the spherical reactor building of Sizewell Nuclear Power Station.

8. The path comes out on the coast road. Cross the road and turn right along a surfaced path parallel to the beach, walking towards Aldeburgh which you can see ahead.

An information board fixed beside the path explains the history of this area called The Haven. The area is now a valuable site for a wide variety of plants. Take the opportunity to explore the area, wandering across the turf and shingle to the shoreline.

On getting close to the town, pass several fishermen's huts behind which you will often see fishing boats drawn up on the beach.

9. Pass the ancient Moot Hall on the right and continue along Crag Path between houses and the shore. Visit, if you have time, the impressive new lifeboat station. Beyond it you will pass the tower of the old lifeboat station and, further on, a similar tower formerly for the coastguards. The lanes off to the right lead to Aldeburgh's wide main street where there are shops and opportunities for refreshment.

Continue along Crag Path beside the beach. Eventually the path ends and you must turn right. Pass Mill House, almost on the edge of the beach, on the left. Immediately after, continue along a gravel path parallel to the shore. Soon the path joins a gravel road leading to Slaughden Quay and the start.

PLACES OF INTEREST NEARBY

The composer Benjamin Britten who lived in Aldeburgh was involved in the Aldeburgh Festival. A visit to the Festival's centre, *Snape Maltings*, in its picturesque setting beside the River Alde, to see the Concert Hall and the associated shops and other facilities is well worth while. About 2 miles northward along the coast is *Thorpeness Windmill*, erected around 100 years ago and now restored and in working order. Open 2pm to 5pm at weekends in May, June and September and daily in July and August.

SIZEWELL AND MINSMERE SLUICE

On this pleasant and varied walk you will pass across arable farmland and rough heathland and through interesting woodland (look out for bats!) before reaching the marshy meadowland of Sizewell Belts Nature Reserve. A farm track and narrow local road lead to Eastbridge. After following a footpath close to the Minsmere River at the edge of the Bird Reserve, the return is along the coast, using the Suffolk Heritage Coast Path.

Minsmere Sluice

The coastal strip between Aldeburgh and Southwold comprises sandy hills covered with woods and heathland, interspersed with low-lying marshes. This is particularly the case in the land immediately north of Sizewell. The Sizewell Nuclear Power Station stands by the shore.

The broad, marshy valley of the Minsmere River, together with wooded slopes to the north, comprise the RSPB's 1,000 acre Minsmere Bird Reserve, which is a nationally known place to see a wide variety of native and migrant birds, especially duck and waders.

Well known and patronised by walkers and birdwatchers is the Eel's Foot pub, situated half way round the walk, at the small and isolated village of Eastbridge. It is a cheerful and welcoming establishment where the menu, displayed on a slatted blackboard, provides a wide range of enjoyable meals. Telephone: 01728 830154. Also, beside the Sizewell car park there is a beach café serving teas and snacks.

- **HOW TO GET THERE:** The tiny settlement of Sizewell lies on the coast about 2 miles east of Leiston. From Leiston High Street, that is the B1122 to Aldeburgh, turn east at the traffic signals and continue for 2 miles to Sizewell beach.
- **PARKING:** There is a free car park right at the end of the road at Sizewell beach.
- **LENGTH OF THE WALK:** 7 miles. Maps: OS Landranger sheet 156 Saxmundham, Aldeburgh and surrounding area; Pathfinder 987 Leiston (GR 475629).

THE WALK

1. from the car park walk back along the road. Just opposite the Vulcan Arms pub, pass an access road to the Sizewell Nuclear Power Station and its Visitors' Centre. Continue along the road and 50 yards after passing a road to Sizewell Hall on the left, turn right along Sandy Lane.

2. About 100 yards before a cottage, turn left along a hedge-lined grassy bridleway, and almost immediately go under the twin electricity grid lines. Before long the path runs beside a wood on the left.

At the end of the wood the lane comes out to an open field; keep straight on. Looking right you will see the extent of the Sizewell Power Station, with its characteristic white domed reactor building. Soon the path becomes a more recognisable cart track through the large field. Occasional trees, gorse and blackberry bushes make it increasingly more like open heath.

3. You come to a gate and, beside it, a high two-step stile. The track continues through an uncultivated area and in 75 yards, just as the

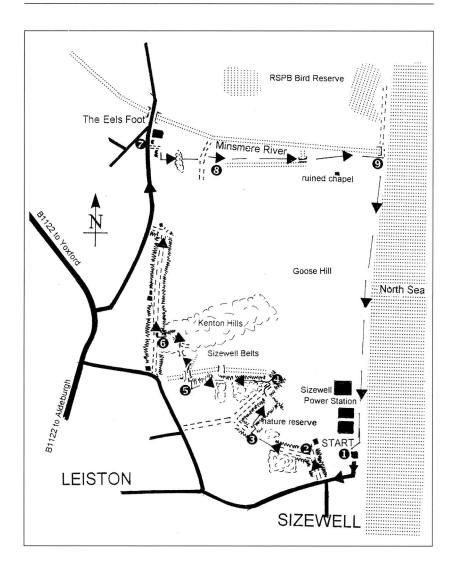

track starts to veer left, turn right along a narrow grass footpath. This is the start of a permissive path through the Sizewell Belts Nature Reserve. In 50 yards turn left into a large meadow.

Go right and cross the meadow to the diagonally opposite corner where, having crossed a stile, you turn right along a leafy lane.

4. Almost where the wood on the left ends, turn left along another

73

grass track, beside the wood. Here and elsewhere you will see bat roosting boxes, usually fixed in threes around tree trunks. They have a narrow slot in the bottom through which bats can squeeze. After walking through the wood come out to an information board about the Sandlings Woodland. Keep straight across a pasture. On the opposite side of the small field go through a belt of woodland to reach a stile leading onto Leiston Common. From here climb slightly, following the edge of the common with bracken on the right. At the top of the rise, skirt a small sandpit. You are overlooking Sizewell Belts, a valley on the right.

5. Look out for a waymark about 50 yards before some prominent trees at the corner of the field, and turn right along a narrow path down the slope into the valley. At the bottom swing left and right to cross a footbridge. At first follow a ditch on the right and, close to a cart bridge over the ditch, turn half left across the meadow towards the trees in the distance.

A footbridge leads you into the wood beside an information board about the 'Historical Landscape'. Come to a delightful small pond which, in early summer, is encompassed with foxgloves of a profuse diversity of shades from dark purple through to creamy white.

Soon after passing the pond come out to a sandy track at right angles and turn left beside a pine wood on the right. Just before the end of the wood, turn left, passing a seat under an oak tree and continue on a well-used path which eventually ends at the Kenton Hills car park. This is the end of the permissive path.

6. Cross the car park, beside the fence on the right, and turn right along a wide, hard track between hedges. In $1/4$ mile pass Upper Abbey Farm. On reaching an almost derelict cottage swing left and in just over 100 yards turn right along a narrow road. Enter Eastbridge and pass Eastbridge Farm on the left.

7. Just before Rose Cottage, the first house on the right, turn right along a lane signed 'Footpath to Minsmere Sluice'. For those requiring refreshment, the Eel's Foot is 200 yards further down the road.

About 50 yards down the lane turn sharp right, beside a hedge on the left, along a narrow footpath which soon makes a left turn and continues along a broad grass strip. Go through a narrow shelter belt of trees and continue along a broad grass way between fields. At the end cross a stile beside a gate and swing half left, to go through a gate and then continue in the same direction as before, between a fence on the left and a ditch on the right. A profusion of wildflowers and grasses grow beside the ditch. Keep straight on at a wooden gate, crossing a stile beside it.

8. The marshy meadows on the left are criss-crossed with drainage ditches and you can see the remains of an old windpump. In the distance, on the left, you can see the row of white-painted former coastguard cottages which stand on the cliff at Dunwich Heath, overlooking Minsmere.

The path bends left and later, on reaching a pair of gate posts, you will have the Minsmere River on the left. Keep beside it for nearly $1/4$ mile to Minsmere Sluice, a new brick structure, where there is an entrance to the Minsmere Bird Reserve.

Walk straight on for a few yards to the edge of the shallow, sandy cliff to see the sea. To return to Sizewell retrace your steps back to the sluice.

9. Take the grass path parallel to the beach towards the power station. This path beside the beach is part of the Suffolk Coast and Heaths Path, a 34 mile route between Felixstowe and Kessingland.

Pass the power station and come to Sizewell Beach Café, the car park and the start of the walk.

PLACES OF INTEREST NEARBY
RSPB's *Minsmere Bird Reserve* includes woods, heathland and wetland habitats. An information centre, shop and tea room are available. Open daily except Tuesdays. Telephone: 01728 648281. *Sizewell Nuclear Power Station Visitors' Centre* offers an exhibition of energy and nuclear power. Open daily from 10 am to 4 pm. Tours by arrangement. Telephone: 01728 642139. *The Long Shop Museum* in Leiston features displays relating to Richard Garrett's steam engines. Open April to October, daily from 10 am to 5 pm (11 am on Sundays). Telephone: 01728 832189.

THE RIVER BLYTH BETWEEN HALESWORTH AND WENHASTON

From the centre of Halesworth, the walk follows firstly a tiny reed-girt stream and then the narrow River Blyth to the hamlet of Mells. A minor road leads through two areas of open heathland to Wenhaston and the nearby Blyford Bridge over the river. The return is beside the river back to Mells and then to Halesworth.

Water lilies on the River Blyth

The River Blyth flows through a broad, shallow valley, eastward from its source near Laxfield to Blythburgh and Southwold. Standing on a little hill, about halfway along the valley, is Halesworth, a small compact town, serving the mainly farming community in the north of Suffolk. Halesworth's winding main street is now bypassed by through vehicles and part of it is traffic free. It is a pleasant place to wander and there are several cafés and pubs offering refreshment at the start or end of the walk.

The route also passes close to the Queen's Head at Blyford. This is a pleasant and popular pub, serving a good range of meals. It stands in an isolated position on the B1123 Southwold road, just opposite Blyford church. Telephone: 01502 478404.

- **HOW TO GET THERE:** Halesworth is in the north-east of Suffolk, 8 miles south of Bungay on the A144 road. From the south, take the A144 from its junction with the A12. The walk starts in the town centre.
- **PARKING:** Waveney District Council Pay and Display town centre car park. Follow the 'P' signs.
- **LENGTH OF THE WALK:** 5½ miles, or 4 miles if you choose to take the short cut, omitting the walk to Blyford Bridge. Maps: OS Landranger sheet 156 Saxmundham, Aldeburgh and surrounding area; Pathfinder 966 Southwold and Halesworth (GR 386775).

THE WALK

1. Start outside the White Hart pub. The pedestrian access to the car park is beside the pub. Walk through the car park to the left-hand corner and take the subway under the main road. Emerge in the park and follow a path which leads to a timber bridge over a stream. Beyond the bridge turn right and pass some picnic tables before going left on a narrow surfaced path to reach a small reed-edged stream, a tributary of the River Blyth. Turn right along the river bank. Cross a stile and continue through a meadow, still keeping beside the stream, which later swings left under the railway. Keep straight on for about 100 yards and then turn left over a stile to go through a very narrow arch bridge.

2. Beyond the bridge, pass a derelict stile and then cross a long timber bridge. Turn left along the edge of a meadow of tall grass, beside a narrow stream. Turn left over a bridge to continue in the same direction but along the opposite bank of the stream through a pleasant hay meadow.

The footpath continues beside the river on the right through a number of small fields. These fields are separated by wide, shallow ditches and in each case there is a long footbridge. After about ¼ mile (and several bridges) you come to a point where the stream makes a right-angle turn to the right. Follow the bank round, and very soon cross yet another bridge. Here turn left, as waymarked, and walk across a grassy meadow. Half left you can see the white painted

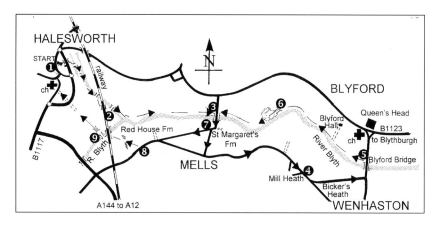

Holton Mill. At the far side of the field you reach the River Blyth.

Cross a timber bridge into another meadow. Pass a wide cart bridge on the right and keep straight on. Continue beside the river, crossing a succession of bridges and stiles, and eventually, at the far corner of a larger field and close to the river on the right, find a narrow footpath through a thicket to a road at Mells.

3. Turn right along the road and cross the river. Bear round to the right and at the road junction turn left opposite Ivy House.

The main route comes back to this point later and so, for a short walk, go right at Ivy House and return to Halesworth, following the description from point 7.

For the full walk, having turned left at Ivy House, walk along the narrow road for about ¼ mile to a junction and turn left towards Wenhaston. These narrow roads are not usually busy but, even so, keep a good look out for vehicles.

Pass Wenhaston Quarry on the left, and later a lane to Watermill Farm. At a road junction, keep straight on through Mill Heath, an interesting area of heathland with heather, bracken and gorse.

4. Soon after a road comes in from the right, pass Harper's Farm and turn left along Low Road beside Bicker's Heath, another common, into Wenhaston. In ¼ mile, turn left towards Blyford and reach the River Blyth at Blyford Bridge. Just ¼ mile further along the road is the Queen's Head pub at Blyford, suitable for halfway refreshment.

5. Immediately beyond the bridge parapet cross a stile on the left and, walking beside a fence on the left, follow the river. At the corner of the field cross a lane which leads to Blyford Hall on the right and continue beside the river along a broad grassy strip. Cross a two-step stile close to the river bank into the corner of the next field and continue to follow the River Blyth as it makes a broad sweep to the right. Pass, on the right, the end of a drainage ditch. When you come to a gate or hurdle at a field corner, go right for 10 yards beside a row of mature trees, to a stile. From the stile cross a bridge to continue straight across the meadow and turn left at the hedge. Cross another stile in the corner which leads to a narrow, slippery path beside the river.

6. In 100 yards cross a long narrow metal footbridge and enter some woods. Follow the narrow footpath, keeping roughly parallel to the river, and emerge from the wood at a stile on the river bank. Continue, following the river and crossing stiles at the field boundaries. On the opposite side of the river you will pass the gravel quarry. Eventually reach the road at Mells and turn left. Cross the river bridge where you were earlier.

7. On reaching Ivy House, keep right along the road signed to Walpole. In $1/4$ mile meet a road coming in from the left, and very soon pass the drive to Red House Farm. About 200 yards further on, opposite a stony track on the left, climb a bank and go over a stile.

8. Take the cross-field path to a gap in the far hedge. Cross the next field, towards the left-hand end of the railway viaduct.

9. Having gone through the railway arch, cross a concrete bridge and go over a paddock to another bridge, into a lane with hedges on both sides. After crossing an access road, keep straight on along a well-used path. After crossing several roads, the path comes out opposite the church. Turn right back to the start.

PLACES OF INTEREST NEARBY
Halesworth and District Museum (local history) is near the church. Open between May and September on Wednesdays and Saturdays from 10 am to 12.30 pm and on Wednesdays, Sundays and bank holidays from 2 pm to 4 pm. Five miles east of Halesworth is 15th-century *Holy Trinity Church, Blythburgh,* one of the finest Perpendicular-style churches in Suffolk.

WALK 17

SOUTHWOLD HARBOUR AND BUSS CREEK

❧❧

The bustling jetties and colourful moorings of Southwold Harbour form the setting for the first ¹/₂ mile of this walk, which starts close to the mouth of the River Blyth. Beyond the river bridge, which gives access to Walberswick, the walk cuts away from the Blyth and follows Buss Creek, a narrow watercourse across the marshes. The walk reaches the sea to the north of Southwold and returns along the seaside promenades and scenic clifftop paths.

Southwold Harbour

Southwold is a delightful coastal resort close to the estuary of the River Blyth. Similar to Aldeburgh, in its isolated position on the coast away from the main road network, it is a quiet town.

A number of coastal inshore fishing boats operate from the harbour. In addition, many sailing craft visit and use the harbour.

The Harbour Inn, passed on the walk, is an interesting old

building with bars on two levels. Specialising in fish, the wide range of starters includes dishes based on prawns, shrimps and anchovies. Main courses such as monkfish with asparagus and noodles, Harbour Inn fish pie and traditional fish and chips are on offer. Telephone: 01502 722381. Among several other pubs and cafés in Southwold is Buckenham's Coffee House, close to the main square and almost opposite the Town Hall, specialising, as its name implies, in coffee and serving lunches and teas. Telephone: 01502 723273.

- **HOW TO GET THERE:** From the A12 about ½ mile north of Blythburgh follow the A1095 to Southwold. Go through the town centre and continue straight on to Southwold Harbour.
- **PARKING:** The walk starts at the Pay and Display car park at the seaward end of Southwold Harbour, by the new lifeboat station.
- **LENGTH OF THE WALK:** 4½ miles. Maps: OS Landranger sheet 156 Saxmundham, Aldeburgh and surrounding area; Pathfinder 966 Southwold and Halesworth (GR 504749).

THE WALK

1. From the car park, walk beside the Blyth Estuary on your left, away from the North Sea coast. Pass on your left the landing stage for the passenger ferry to Walberswick, which operates generally at weekends. Continue along the harbour road.

Pass on the right the Southwold Boatyard, Chandlery and Tearoom and soon reach the Harbour Inn.

2. As you pass, notice the plaque on the wall indicating the height of the flood in 1953. After the inn, keep straight on close to the river, and then climb to the top of the flood protection wall.

3. Before long reach a bridge across the river which is on the site of a former bridge which carried the Southwold Railway line. At the bridge go straight on over a stile, continuing, at first, beside the river but almost immediately the river bends away left and the path continues beside Buss Creek, a narrow watercourse. In about 100 yards, pass a sluice gate across the creek. Keep along the path on a raised bank, beside the creek, which soon becomes almost covered with reeds and rushes. The path is circling the town of Southwold.

4. Cross the remains of a stile at a field boundary and still keep

81

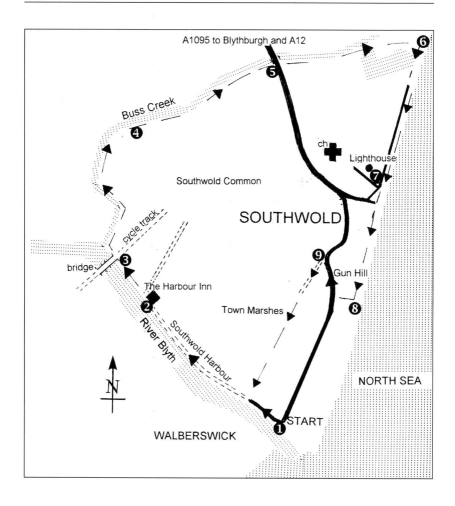

along the river wall. In a further 200 yards or so cross another stile and then at a four-way footpath sign cross a path at right angles and keep straight on beside a deeper and wider watercourse.

5. After some time the path comes out onto Mights Road, the A1095, the road into Southwold. You may pause to rest on a public seat beside the water here. Cross straight over the road and continue in the same direction as before, at first through a plantation of willows.

A path comes in from some houses 200 yards away on the right but keep straight on. You are walking towards a distant row of multicoloured beach huts which front the beach. Soon you are walking between the creek on the left and a lake on the right.

6. The path ends at a beachside car park. Turn right and walk between the car park and the Southwold Model Boat Pond. At the end of the car park, cross the road and pass the former pier buildings on the left. Continue along a footpath at the top of the cliff.

7. On reaching a triangular green on the right, where a large mast stands, flanked by two cannons, pause. This is St James Green, a former site of the coastguard station. If you have time, take the opportunity of exploring this part of the town by going right along St James Green. Pass the lighthouse and keep straight on to the parish church. Having seen the pleasant greens, flanked by old houses, make your way back to St James Green, passing beside Adnams Brewery.

On returning to the coast, turn right along the top of the cliff, and where the road swings half right keep along the footpath at the cliff top, soon to pass the Southwold Sailors Reading Room (1864).

Still keep along the path and reach a grassed area off to the right. Continue straight on. The path drops and then climbs steeply up to Gun Hill, an extensive green where six old cannons are sited.

8. Beyond the guns, after passing the Lifeboat Museum, the footpath bends right and leads out in 50 yards to a road. Turn right and follow the road for about 200 yards.

9. Where the road bends right at a junction, make almost a U-turn to the left at a footpath sign to walk along a broad cart track beside a ditch on the right. The path eventually leads out to the road at Southwold Harbour. Turn left back to the start.

PLACES OF INTEREST NEARBY

Southwold Museum in Victoria Street houses interesting displays of local history. Open between Easter and September daily from 2.30 pm to 4.30 pm. Telephone: 01502 722375. On Gun Hill is the *Southwold Lifeboat Museum.* Open between Spring Bank Holiday and September daily from 2.30 pm to 4.30 pm.

OULTON BROAD AND
THE RIVER WAVENEY

*Carlton Marshes has much to offer the wildlife enthusiast:
information boards describe the habitat and name some of the
plants which may be seen. After passing through lush vegetation, this
walk crosses the marshes to the bank of the Waveney where you can
enjoy fine views before returning to picturesque Oulton Broad.*

Oulton Broad

For most of its length the River Waveney forms the northern
boundary of Suffolk. Navigable from Beccles through Breydon Water
to the Rivers Yare and Bure, the Waveney forms part of the network
of lakes and waterways known as the Norfolk Broads. It is linked,
via the Oulton Dyke, to Oulton Broad.

On both sides of the river are low-lying marshy areas which, for
the most part, have been drained and provide good grazing for
animals, especially in summer. However, there are wet, marshy

sections, such as Carlton Marshes owned by the Suffolk Wildlife Trust. The Trust asks visitors to refrain from using the path on the bank by Oulton Dyke during the nesting season; i.e. between 1st April and 31st July, to avoid disturbing some of the rarer species such as marsh harriers who nest close by. An alternative route is therefore described for the late spring and early summer.

Away from the walk route but well worth visiting is the Swan at Barnby, a popular pub specialising in a wide variety of fish dishes. It will be found 3 miles towards Beccles, just off the A146. Telephone: 01502 476646. There are also a number of pubs, restaurants and cafés in Lowestoft.

- **HOW TO GET THERE:** From Oulton Broad, go 1 mile along the A146 road towards Beccles. At the edge of the town, look out for a brown 'Wildlife Centre' sign and turn right along Burnt Hill Lane for $1/_4$ mile to the Information Centre and car park.
- **PARKING:** There is a good car park at the Suffolk Wildlife Trust's Information Centre.
- **LENGTH OF THE WALK:** 4 miles for the full walk to Oulton Broad; otherwise $2^1/_2$ miles. OS Landranger sheet 134 Norwich and The Broads; Pathfinder 925 Lowestoft and Beccles (North) (GR 508920).

THE WALK

1. Leave the car park at the pedestrian exit and turn right for 10 yards along the lane. Go through the pedestrian gate on the left and follow the gravel path beside the hedge on the left. Before long the path swings right with an attractive reedy ditch on the left. Leave the field at a gate and continue along the gravel path through a rough, marshy meadow. After another gate the path passes through even lusher vegetation with reeds and willowherb.

2. Leave the gravel path, turning left, to cross a wide ditch on a timber footbridge. From the bridge keep straight on, walking now a narrower grass path through tall vegetation. Before long swing round to the right. Through a gap in a hedge on the left you will espy Sprat's Water.

In rather less than 200 yards come to a small rectangular pond surrounded by many bog-loving plants. A path off to the left here leads to another view of Sprat's Water. Continue straight on and before long come to a boardwalk. Do not take the walkway over the

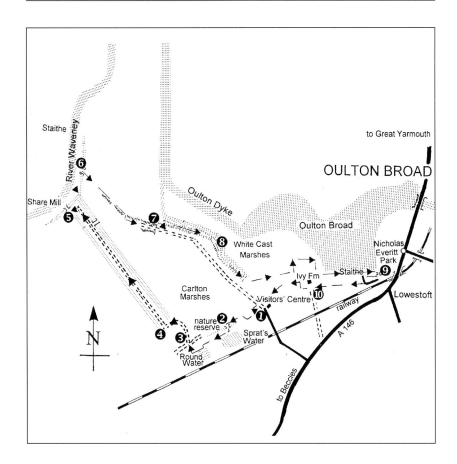

bridge to the right, but go straight on along the timber walkway which, after bending left, ends at the edge of Round Water. Step off the boardwalk to the right and follow the narrow grass way, at first beside the lake but soon circling right through the fen to come out at a junction of wide paths.

3. Walk straight ahead along a 6 foot wide grass cart track going north. The track bends gradually round to the left and comes to a gate leading into a field.

4. Turn sharp right, and continue along the straight cart track with a narrow reed filled ditch on the left and a broad open watercourse on the right. In ½ mile pass a substantial footbridge on the right.

5. About 200 yards further on, bend left and right, dropping slightly to cross a steel bridge over a drainage ditch and climb steps onto the bank of the River Waveney. There are bits of old concrete structures here beside the river which are probably the remains of Share Mill shown on the Ordnance Survey map.

Turn right along the riverside path. This is part of the Angles Way, a long-distance path through the Waveney Valley.

6. Having walked about 300 yards alongside the river, you come to a point where the path leaves the bank down steps on the right.

Before descending, go left onto a narrow band of grass at the river's edge. Here is a good view of the River Waveney. On the right, $1/4$ mile downstream on the opposite bank, is a staithe where boats are moored.

Continuing the walk, from the steps keep on a narrow path through reeds. In well over $1/4$ mile, come to a sign where the path goes right for a few yards and over a stile into a meadow. Turn left and follow the edge of the field on the left.

At the corner of the field go through a gate and in 10 yards negotiate a pair of steel hurdles which lead to a good cart track. Having gone through another gate you come to a hard farm road.

7. Here turn left and climb a bank up to a footpath sign and have a good look at the surrounding marshes. From this point the public footpath runs on this bank for almost a mile to Oulton Broad.

The Suffolk Wildlife Trust requests people not to use the path during the nesting season because shy and rare birds inhabit the reedbeds beside the path. Moreover the path is sometimes overgrown. Should it be the nesting season, retrace your steps back to the farm road and walk along it, back to the car park. (See note at the end about the path from the car park to Oulton Broad.)

For most of the year, the main walk continues from the footpath sign at the top of the bank along a narrow path between bushes. Cross a stile and continue along the bank, which is a flood protection barrier for the grazing marshes on the right.

8. The path bends round to the right and after crossing a stile comes to a sign saying 'White Cast Marshes'. Nearby pass a two-way footpath sign. From this point, a footpath goes half right back to the Information Centre. For the main walk, keep along the flood protection bank, which before long turns left.

In the next ¼ mile there are several bends but the path gets wider and soon there are distant views of Oulton Broad. Pass 'Broad View Caravans' on the right and come to a marina. Walk straight on along the concrete quay with Broads' cruisers ranged alongside. Continue, passing more berths, until you reach a macadam surfaced path and enter Nicholas Everitt Park.

9. In a few yards, at a junction of paths, turn right and cross a timber footbridge. Immediately after the bridge turn right along a stony path, passing 'Pets Corner' on the left, and then go through a picnic area and out to an access road.

Turn left along the road and in 100 yards, where the road bends left, turn right at a sign 'Public Footpath to Burnt Hill Lane'. The path starts as a narrow path between hedges. You then cross an access to a caravan site. Keep in the same direction, following a hedge on the right and crossing several stiles en route.

10. Cross straight over an access road to Ivy Farm on the right. Keep the fence on the right through the next field and then, after a stile, turn right. The path eventually bends round to the left and you are back at the Suffolk Wildlife Trust Information Centre and the start.

Note: For anyone who did not use the footpath along the bank beside White Cast Marshes, a walk to Oulton Broad from the Information Centre is quite easy. From the corner of the car park go east and follow the well-signed path for about ½ mile.

PLACES OF INTEREST NEARBY
The East Anglia Transport Museum is at Chapel Road, Carlton Colville (1 mile towards Beccles on the A146). The collection includes trams and trolley buses in operation. Open between Spring Bank Holiday and September on Saturdays 2 pm to 4 pm, Sundays 11 am to 5 pm; also daily in August. The 17th-century Broad House in Nicholas Everitt Park at Oulton Broad houses *The Lowestoft Museum.* Open between Spring Bank Holiday and September or Mondays to Saturdays from 10 am to 5 pm, Sundays 2 pm to 5 pm. (April, May and October, weekend afternoons only). Telephone: 01502 511457.

BRANDON AND THE LITTLE OUSE RIVER

This lovely peaceful walk follows the Little Ouse Path beside the winding river from Brandon to Santon Downham, a small village in the heart of Thetford Forest, and there is the opportunity to continue further along the riverside if you wish. The return is pleasant along a grassy forest path.

The Little Ouse River

Breckland is an area of dry, light, sandy soil extending over nearly 400 square miles of north-west Suffolk and west Norfolk. Brandon, a Breckland town, lies beside a bridge over the Little Ouse River, which in ancient times was the first crossing point of the river.

Underneath the capping of Breckland's sandy soil lies flinty chalk and this is the basis of Brandon's traditional industry of mining and processing flints. The industrial history of the town is displayed at the Brandon Heritage Centre.

Conveniently situated for the walk is Collins' Fish Restaurant in Brandon High Street. As its name implies, it serves a good range of fried fish dishes whilst also offering chicken and steak. The menu includes a selection of starters and sweets. Telephone: 01842 811766. Brandon also has several public houses serving meals, among them the Ram, just north of the bridge, and the Five Bells on Market Hill.

- **HOW TO GET THERE:** Brandon is on the northern boundary of Suffolk. It is 6 miles from Thetford along the B1107, and 12 miles from Bury St Edmunds on the B1106.
- **PARKING:** Forest Heath District Council's car park, off High Street, north of the Market Square and near the Pioneer supermarket.
- **LENGTH OF THE WALK:** 5$\frac{1}{2}$ miles, with an option for a further 1$\frac{1}{2}$ miles. Maps: OS Landranger sheet 144 Thetford, Breckland and surrounding area: Pathfinder 942 Lakenheath and Brandon and 943 Thetford (GR 783865).

THE WALK

1. From Brandon Market Hill walk northward along High Street and in $\frac{1}{4}$ mile cross the bridge over the Little Ouse River. Take the first turning right, Riverside Way. A waymark denotes that this is the Little Ouse Path, to Thetford. In 50 yards leave the road, turning right beside a fence along a narrow path towards the river.

2. The path swings left at the river bank and immediately crosses a timber bridge over a small tributary. There is a landing stage here at the upper limit of navigation along the river. Soon cross another bridge and continue beside the river.

The narrow path follows the bank of the river for 2$\frac{1}{2}$ miles. The river, on the right, is edged with a wide variety of water-loving plants, while on the left is an expanse of marsh where reeds intermix with willow trees. On rising ground, beyond the reedbeds and willows, can be seen the edge of the conifer forest. In marked contrast, the opposite bank of the river has small, open grassy meadows interspersed with woods.

After about $\frac{3}{4}$ mile, the willows on the left give way to a plantation of tall and mature poplars, but the area is still very marshy. The river has meandered round a number of bends but eventually comes to a $\frac{1}{2}$ mile length of straight river. Here it must have been artificially straightened at some time because the Suffolk

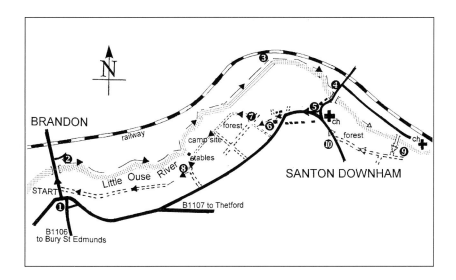

county boundary still winds about along the river's former course.

3. From the end of the straight section, the river makes a gentle sweep round to the right. You may see, 100 yards away on the left, the Norwich to Ely railway line.

4. Eventually you come to a girder bridge over the river. Climb steps and turn right over the road bridge to enter Santon Downham.

A footbridge crosses the river a further ½ mile upstream and it would be possible to extend the walk from point 4. To do so, continue beside the Little Ouse on a permissive path as far as the footbridge (point 9 on map), then cross the river and in 200 yards turn right along a forest track for about ½ mile to meet a road (point 10 on map) at the edge of Santon Downham.

Continuing the main walk from the road bridge, pass a terrace of attractive flint-faced bungalows on the right and, soon after, pass the Forest Enterprises HQ, the car park and village shop.

5. Almost opposite St Mary's church, at a road junction, turn right towards Brandon. In ¼ mile where the road makes a sharpish bend left, indicated by a chevron sign, leave the road, going straight on along a surfaced drive in front of houses on the right.

6. On reaching the village hall and the last house on the right, follow a narrow grass footpath straight on into the forest. The path soon gets wider as it continues through attractive mixed woodland until it bends half right to join a path from the left.

7. In 100 yards or so, cross over a sandy track and continue along a grassy path. Pass an iron barrier to stop vehicles and follow the path round to the left. Gently curving through the forest, this well-used path passes several grassy glades which comprise the County Council's Forest Camp Site.

To see the river again, look out for a path to the right which leads along a slatted walkway to a fishing platform 50 yards away, on the river bank. You must, however, return to the path.

Pass a junction with a track to the left and keep straight on. There is a notice about the camp site here. Pass another metal barrier to leave the forest and continue along a flinty track, passing the stables and paddocks of a riding school on the right.

8. Where the track bends left and the woods start again on the right, leave the track and turn right along a narrow footpath between the wood on the left and a wire fence on the right.

Before long there are fences both sides of the path, and the footpath gradually widens to a cart track. An old flint-faced wall is on the left. This track is called Gas House Drove, and goes to the High Street. A path on the right just before the end leads directly to the Pioneer store and the car park. Turn left along High Street, to return to Market Hill and the start.

PLACES OF INTEREST NEARBY

Described as the oldest industrial site in Europe, parts of the neolithic flint mines *Grimes Graves* have been excavated and visitors may descend one of the shafts to see the galleries where flints were mined 4,000 years ago. They are located 4 miles north-east of Brandon; follow the A1065 for 2 miles and turn right. Open daily from April to October, and Wednesday through to Sunday for the remainder of the year. *Brandon Heritage Centre* gives an insight into the Brandon flint industry from neolithic times to the present day. The displays also cover other aspects of the town. Open April to October on Saturdays from 10.30 am to 5 pm and Sundays from 2 pm to 5 pm. Telephone: 01842 813707.

WALK 20

THE RIVER LARK AT MILDENHALL

From the historic town centre of Mildenhall, the walk goes westward on cross-field paths. On reaching a leafy lane beside the River Lark, the route turns along the north bank of the river to reach Kings Staunch Cottage. After passing Wamil Hall, you return on a riverside path through delightful meadows.

The River Lark

Mildenhall stands at the western boundary of Suffolk. Land to the west of the town drops down a few feet to the flat Cambridgeshire Fens. The River Lark skirts the southern side of the town.

Because of flooding in the Fens, particularly in 1957, a new watercourse, called the Cut-Off Channel, was built from the River Lark at Mildenhall, along the contour, connecting with the Rivers Little Ouse and Wissey and discharging floodwaters to the Great Ouse much nearer the sea. A large air base adjoins the town.

There are several cafés and pubs in Mildenhall, among them the *Riverside Hotel* which serves bar meals in a comfortable lounge lined with books and decorated with many interesting prints. The light and airy restaurant looks out over a lawn stretching down to the river. Telephone: 01638 717274.

- **HOW TO GET THERE:** Mildenhall is a small town a mile off the A11, the London to Norwich road, about 9 miles north east of Newmarket. From the large roundabout on the A11, take the A1101 to the centre of Mildenhall.
- **PARKING:** Turn at the war memorial into King Street. At the end turn left to the car park not far from the swimming pool and the Jubilee Centre.
- **LENGTH OF THE WALK:** 3½ miles (short cut possible). Maps: OS Landranger sheet 143 Ely, Wisbech and surrounding area; Pathfinder 962 Mildenhall and Fordham (GR 712745).

THE WALK

1. From the car park go out to King Street and walk towards the A1101 main road. Pass the Mildenhall Museum, an old flint-faced building, on the left and then turn left down Market Street.

2. Reaching the Market Place, pass the old pump and the ancient wooden, open hexagonal Market Cross. Cross High Street and, going left for a few yards, walk along Church Walk, a footpath passing the church. Beyond the churchyard keep straight on along a narrow road.

At the end of the road, go straight on along a lane with fences on both sides and pass some bungalows on the left. Beyond the housing estate continue through a playing field, passing the school buildings on the right.

3. Leave the playing field by a gate and continue straight on along a narrow cross-field path for about 100 yards. Then in mid-field turn left on another cross-field path and at the end descend a steep bank to meet a well-used track.

4. The full walk goes right from this point, to return here after looping round Wamil Hall. The walk can therefore be shortened, if you wish, by crossing the track, turning left and following the river bank.

Having turned right for the full walk, continue along the narrow leafy lane with a hedge on the right and a narrow tree belt on the

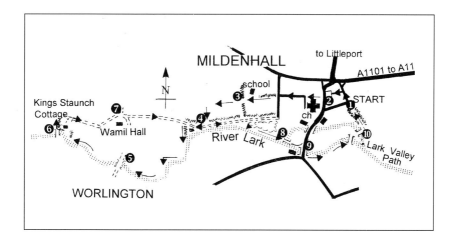

left which slopes down to the river about 10 yards away. Pass a white bungalow on the left and just beyond it, when you reach an open field, leave the track turning left beside the hedge. At the river bank, continue beside the river on the left, round the field.

5. In about ½ mile there is a cart bridge crossing the river. Climb a steep ramp to the level of the bridge, cross the gravel track to continue through a meadow, keeping beside the river. Half left you will see the tower of Worlington church.

At the opposite end of the meadow cross a stile leading into the corner of an arable field. Still keeping the river on the left, follow the edge of the field. In a little over 200 yards come to a kissing gate set in a tall, thick hedge, which leads into a beautiful riverside garden.

6. The way is through the garden, between the river and Kings Staunch Cottage on the right. Leave the garden by another kissing gate and turn right beside the hedge for 50 yards.

Reach a grassy lane and turn right beside a tall garden wall on the right. Very soon come to the drive to the house. Keep along the drive and in about 300 yards go through a gateway with double wooden gates.

7. On the right is a curved brick wall and the entrance to Wamil Hall. Go straight on and in 50 yards where the farm drive bends right, take the cart track straight on towards Mildenhall church in the distance. Soon there are open fields on both sides of the track and at the far side the track enters a lane and passes the white bungalow on the right. This is where you were walking earlier. Follow the lane to the point close to a telephone pole, where the footpath used earlier goes up a bank on the left.

Go right for a few yards and continue along the river bank with a wood on the left. Come out to a cricket field and continue beside the River Lark on the right.

8. Under a great ash tree, keep straight on and in 50 yards go right on a bridge over an arm of the river which feeds water to Lark Mills. Continue along the riverside footpath, passing some attractive flint-faced buildings on the opposite bank. Immediately before the road bridge, turn left and climb up to road level.

9. Turn right, cross the bridge, and immediately turn left along a gravel track, passing Riverside Cottage. Soon pass Gasspool Sluice, an automatic sluice gate with, beside it, a dam across the river. Keep along the river bank on a crushed stone path. In 200 yards take the wooden bridge over the river and then a path through a narrow tree belt.

10. Cross another bridge which takes you over the tail race from the mill. Here, on the right, the Lark Valley Path runs through a pleasant meadow where there are several seats, on its route upstream towards Bury St Edmunds (12 miles away).

The walk goes leftish from the bridge and along a lane which, after passing a supermarket on the left, leads straight back to the Jubilee Centre and the car park.

PLACES OF INTEREST NEARBY
The exhibits at *Mildenhall and District Museum* include a display of the natural history of Breckland and the story of the Mildenhall Air Base. Open, except Mondays and Tuesdays, daily, 2.30 pm to 4.30 pm, also Friday mornings from 11 am. Telephone: 01638 716970. About 6 miles along the A1101 towards Bury St Edmunds is *West Stow Country Park*, and *Anglo-Saxon village* where several ancient dwellings have been reconstructed. Open daily from 10 am to 4.15 pm. Telephone: 01284 728718.